My Travels with Mrs. Kennedy

My Travels with Mrs. Kennedy

CLINT HILL
and LISA McCUBBIN HILL

GALLERY BOOKS

NEW YORK   LONDON   TORONTO   SYDNEY   NEW DELHI

Gallery Books
An Imprint of Simon & Schuster, LLC
1230 Avenue of the Americas
New York, NY 10020

First Gallery Books trade paperback edition April 2024

GALLERY BOOKS and colophon are registered trademarks of Simon & Schuster, LLC

Simon & Schuster: Celebrating 100 Years of Publishing in 2024

For information about special discounts for bulk purchases, please contact Simon & Schuster Special Sales
at 1-866-506-1949 or business@simonandschuster.com.

The Simon & Schuster Speakers Bureau can bring authors to your live event. For more information or to book an event,
contact the Simon & Schuster Speakers Bureau at 1-866-248-3049 or visit our website at www.simonspeakers.com.

Interior design by Matt Ryan

Manufactured in the United States of America

10 9 8 7 6 5 4 3 2 1

Library of Congress Cataloging-in-Publication Data is available for the hardcover.

ISBN 978-1-9821-8111-6
ISBN 978-1-9821-8112-3 (pbk)
ISBN 978-1-9821-8113-0 (ebook)

To Chris, Corey,
Connor, and Cooper

CONTENTS

PREFACE

When I look at these photographs of Mrs. Kennedy as we traveled through Europe and Asia and South America, I realize now what a privilege it was to have been part of those private, joyful moments she experienced. There we were, all over the globe, in some of the most exotic countries in the world, sharing laughs, living through some crazy adventures. When you travel with someone—particularly in foreign countries—you experience things that can't be fully appreciated by anyone who wasn't there.

I hope you enjoy these travels with Mrs. Kennedy as much as she and I did.

1

———

THE TRUNK

———

ALEXANDRIA, VIRGINIA, 2019

It all started with the discovery of the trunk.

Lisa McCubbin and I were standing in the garage of the home I had owned since 1967 at 1068 North Chambliss Street in Alexandria, Virginia. It was a crisp September afternoon in 2019, and we were into our third day of sorting through the mountains of stuff I had accumulated in my eighty-seven years of life. I hadn't lived in the house for nearly a decade and had finally decided it was time to sell.

"What's in here?" Lisa asked.

"I have no idea," I said. "I haven't opened it in more than fifty years."

The oversized steamer trunk was barely visible, sitting on the cement floor of the dank garage, shoved against a shelf filled with rusty gardening tools, its white-stenciled block letters peering out beneath a box that claimed to have a Craftsman wet/dry vac in it.

Lisa lifted the bulky cardboard box that did indeed contain a lightweight vacuum, and as she put it aside, the black metal steamer trunk revealed itself. I stood over it, and without warning, a sudden wave of memories flooded my brain. India, Pakistan, Paris, Greece, Morocco, three glorious weeks on the Amalfi coast.

It was more impressive than I remembered. Trimmed in brass with a heavy lock to keep its contents safe, the two-inch white lettering on the lid boldly declared to whom it belonged.

CLINTON HILL
THE WHITE HOUSE
WASHINGTON D.C.

We both stood there, silent, staring at it for a moment, and then Lisa said, "It's just as you always described it." She paused, looked at me, and asked, "May I open it?"

"Let's wait until tomorrow," I said. "It's getting late. And you better have some rubber gloves. Whatever is in there is more than likely covered with mold and God knows what else."

I shuddered to think of the disgusting mess that must be inside. "Years ago, the garage flooded after a heavy rain. It was up to here," I said, holding one hand at my waist. "It's probably crawling with worms and big black spiders."

"Oh God!" Lisa grimaced. "Did you have to say that? Now I'll have nightmares. But you're right. Let's get back to the hotel and we'll start fresh tomorrow. I can hardly wait."

"Don't get your hopes up," I said. "If there's anything salvageable, it's probably just junk, like all the rest of the stuff in here."

The trunk

I had been procrastinating dealing with the house at 1068 because, frankly, the thought of cleaning it out was overwhelming. I had long since taken out everything I needed, or thought was of value, and I would have been happy to call 1-800-GOT-JUNK to go in and clear the place out.

"What about your medal?" Lisa had reminded me. "It must be there somewhere. You don't want to see it on eBay or, worse, have it end up in a dumpster. It's too important."

On December 3, 1963, I had been honored with the U.S. Treasury Department's highest civilian award for bravery. There were photos of the ceremony, even a video of it now on YouTube, but the medal had never meant anything to me. I never wanted it, never thought I deserved it. I didn't see myself as brave. I was just doing my job. As a Secret Service agent on the White House Detail, I had trained for that moment. Trained to jump into the line of fire, to be a human shield for the president, the first lady, or whomever we were assigned to protect. But I would never get over the feeling that if only I had reacted a little bit quicker—one second, or maybe half a second—I wouldn't be here, and there'd be no damn medal. After all these years, I honestly didn't know where it was. But Lisa finally convinced me that it would be better for us to go through everything ourselves rather than have some strangers deciding what was trash and what was history. The medal was really the only thing we were looking for.

We were staying at the Willard InterContinental in Washington, D.C., about a twenty-minute drive from the house in Alexandria. Lisa and I had been traveling almost constantly for the previous several years—whether conducting research for a book, promoting a book with media and speaking engagements, or, more rarely, traveling for pleasure. We made it a habit to visit the D.C. area three or four times a year. We'd have lunch with my two sons, Chris and Corey, and their families, who still lived nearby, and we'd catch up with friends—and it had become our routine to stay at the Willard. The historic hotel was centrally located to familiar restaurants where we'd meet friends—mostly other former Secret Service agents and their wives —and it was just across 15th Street from the White House complex where I attended an annual meeting of the Special Agents in Charge of Presidential Protection each December. At Christmastime, the hotel lobby was decorated with miles of festive garland and a towering Christmas tree covered in white lights, red bows, and an enviable selection of the collectible White House Christmas ornaments produced by the White House Historical Association.

The first time we stayed at the Willard, I was offered an upgrade to a suite, which I happily accepted. The bellman took us up to the fourth floor, and as we exited the elevators, he turned right and said, "Here you are. This is a very special suite, Mr. Hill. I think you'll enjoy it."

On the door was a brass plaque:

John F. Kennedy Suite
410

Lisa and I looked at each other but didn't say anything as the bellman opened the door and led us into the spacious suite. Hanging on the wall in the entry was a painting of JFK—a reproduction of the Aaron Shikler painting of him with his head down, arms crossed, deep in thought. The same one that hangs in the White House.

At the end of our stay that first time, Lisa wrote a note to the general manager thanking him for the lovely hospitality and explained why the John F. Kennedy suite really was particularly meaningful to me. From that point on, whenever we were in Washington, we stayed at the Willard, and if it was available, they would put is in Room 410.

The following morning, we returned to the house at 1068 North Chambliss Street, armed with several pairs of rubber gloves and a fresh supply of Hefty garbage bags. Lisa could hardly contain her excitement to see what was inside the trunk.

"I want to videotape it," she said. "I feel like we're opening up Tutankhamun's tomb."

She slipped the purple rubber gloves over each hand, up to her elbows, and handed me her iPhone. "I'll open the trunk, and you hold the camera," she said.

"Yes, Madam Director," I said. "Are you sure you trust me to record this?"

"Just push the red button and keep it focused on the trunk," she said, laughing. "Okay, go."

I pushed the red button and she slowly opened the lid.

It was packed to the brim, with just the top layer immediately visible: some manila envelopes stuffed full and closed with clasps, and dozens of boxes, all shapes and sizes. There looked to be bigger boxes underneath. Many of the items were covered with black, dusty mold, and an overpowering smell of mildew and mustiness wafted out like the trunk was exhaling after holding its breath for the last five decades, but overall, it was in much better shape than I had expected.

"Well, just start pulling things out," I said. "Let's see what we've got."

One by one, she began opening the flimsy cardboard gift-type boxes to see what was inside. There were crystal paperweights; Air Force One playing cards still in their original plastic seals; dozens of individual boxes containing blue and gold tie bars, cuff link sets, and Zippo lighters emblazoned with the presidential seal.

"Presidential gifts," I said. "We used to give those out like candy when we traveled. All different kinds of crap. Nothing of any consequence."

There were dozens and dozens, perhaps more than a hundred little assorted boxes. Plastic, velvet, cardboard. Any one of them could contain the medal. Or not.

"Okay. Go ahead and turn off the video," Lisa said. "I'll stay out here and sort through everything. It's going to take me a while to open all these boxes. Why don't you go back inside and continue going through the stuff in your office?"

The task before us still seemed daunting to me, and I was grateful that Lisa was taking charge. "Sounds good to me," I said.

I walked back through the door that led from the garage to the basement. My "office" was really just a corner of the basement where I had a big government-style desk, surrounded by filing cabinets and shelves overflowing with cardboard boxes—some labeled, most not. A stairway leading to the main level of the house cut the basement in half. At the far end of my corner office was a large laundry room with a washer and dryer, a utility sink, an old refrigerator that didn't work, and half a dozen floor-to-ceiling shelving units stacked with more boxes and bags. So much stuff. Was my medal even down here? Where to even begin?

As I glanced around the laundry room, my eyes landed on a glass casserole dish that appeared to be sitting on top of some framed pictures. I picked up the dish, and lying there staring up at me was President Harry S. Truman. A black-and-white photo of the thirty-third president of the United States in a silver frame, and it appeared to be autographed in blue ink. I pulled my glasses out of my chest pocket and put them on so I could read the inscription.

To Clint J. Hill
Harry Truman 3-13-68

I'd met President Truman a couple of times, but I couldn't recall the occasion of him signing this photograph. Underneath the Truman photo was a framed photo of President Eisenhower.

For Clint Hill
With deep appreciation of his work at the White House—and with best wishes
Dwight D. Eisenhower

A larger frame, about eleven by fourteen, lay facedown underneath Ike's. *And who's this?* I flipped it over. And there she was.

For Clinton Hill — with memories of all you did to make the White House years all that they were for President Kennedy and for me.
With my deepest gratitude
Jacqueline Kennedy

C·J·H

Dressed in an elegant strapless ball gown, white gloves up past her elbows, a tiara holding her thick brown hair back from her face accentuating her wide-set eyes. She stood in between her husband and France's minister of culture, André Malraux, with Malraux's wife barely visible behind. She was smiling with delight, like she'd just made eye contact with someone she adored and hadn't seen in a long time. The black-and-white photo was in a beautiful sterling silver frame in desperate need of polishing, with a gold presidential seal at the top and my initials, C.J.H., engraved at the bottom.

This photo too was autographed.

For Clinton Hill—with memories of all you did to make the
White House years all that they were for President Kennedy and for me.
With my deepest gratitude
Jacqueline Kennedy

It was an interesting photo because President John F. Kennedy and Malraux, dressed in tuxedos, and Mrs. Malraux, tucked behind her husband, were all looking away. Mrs. Kennedy was the only one looking right at you, with that dazzling smile, so all you really noticed was her.

I was lost in thought, holding the frame in my two hands, when Lisa came walking in from the garage.

"What's that?" she asked. "Anything interesting?"

I waited for her to get close, to see for herself. She stood next to me, and as she read the inscription, she put her arm around me and gently caressed my back.

"What a beautiful gift. Do you remember when she gave this to you?"

"Yeah. I do." I could see her standing there, her eyes glistening as I opened the box and read what she had written. "It was when I left her in November 1964."

"So, going through all of this stuff must bring back a lot of memories."

"Sure it does," I replied. "Some good, some not so good. But lots of things I haven't thought about for a long time."

"What does this photo remind you of? Do you remember when it was taken?"

I looked down at the photograph in my hands and laughed. "Oh, I remember, all right," I said. "That's André Malraux, the French minister of culture. This was taken at the White House during a dinner held in honor of Malraux. Must have been in 1962. This was the night she convinced Malraux to loan the *Mona Lisa* to the United States. She had a special connection with Malraux, and boy did she use her feminine charm on him that night. It was the first time the French government had ever let the *Mona Lisa* leave France. And that was all her doing. It was remarkable, really.

"And it all started when we were in Paris."

2

———

PARIS

———

1961

Four months into her role as first lady, Mrs. Kennedy accompanied her husband on a historic European trip that began with three days in Paris.

I had flown to Paris a week ahead of the presidential party to do the advance, and as we worked through the millions of logistics, protocol, and security details, it was clear that the people of France were tremendously excited about welcoming the new American president on his first official trip to Europe and were intent on creating a grand impression. But what surprised me was the extraordinary interest there was in Mrs. Kennedy. The French officials insisted that the public would be extremely disappointed if there weren't plenty of opportunities to see *la belle Jacqui*, along with the handsome *président Américain*. I could not recall such fascination with any previous first ladies.

One of the biggest concerns I had about the Paris trip was the tightness of the packed schedule. From arrival in Paris on May 31 to departure for Vienna on June 3, 1961, Mrs. Kennedy would constantly be on the go with little time for rest. In addition, time had to be allotted for her to "freshen up" and change clothes between events. Much had been made in the press about Mrs. Kennedy's wardrobe—whether she would wear French or American designs—and she had taken great care to choose appropriate, but eye-catching, ensembles.

Fortunately, taking care of the many steamer trunks filled with daytime suits and dresses, evening gowns, and all the matching shoes, handbags, and hats was not my responsibility.

But while the media was focused on every little nuance of her apparel, what they missed was the critical role she was playing in international diplomacy.

Hundreds of thousands of people lined the streets of Paris to witness President and Mrs. Kennedy's arrival in a grand ceremonial parade. One hundred French motorcycle policemen led the motorcade into the heart of Paris, a 101-gun salute commenced as the procession entered the Porte D'Orléans at a cadence of six shots a minute, and then, as the motorcade traveled down Boulevard Saint-Michel, onto Rue de Rivoli and along the Tuileries Garden, the sounds of the motorcycles were overpowered by a vociferous chorus of attention-seeking screams. If you can imagine, all along the route, men dressed in suits, ladies in skirts and heels, even children wearing their Sunday best, yelling, whooping, and hollering at the tops of their lungs: *"Vive le président Kennedy!"* and *"Vive Jac-qui! Vive Jac-qui!"* The sheer joy and enthusiasm were staggering. As the parade entered the Place des Pyramides, the motorcycles parted and waiting, in perfect formation, were a hundred Republican Guards on horseback. Row after row of the beautiful mounts, with their riders in full ceremonial uniform, marching in unison leading the rest of the way to the Quai d'Orsay. It was a magnificent show of splendor, steeped in history and tradition—the kind of pageantry Mrs. Kennedy adored.

The French provided a new Citroën auto with a plexiglass roof, designed specifically for her so the public could see her as she rode through the city. Even though the interior was not as large as she was used to, she never made a complaint. From the moment she arrived, I could tell that she felt very much at home in Paris and was so happy to be there, speaking the language she loved. I knew of course that she spoke French and had spent a year in France during her college years, but when she began conversing effortlessly with both President and Mrs. de Gaulle, I realized how truly fluent she was. The U.S. State Department had supplied an excellent translator for President Kennedy, but oftentimes it was Mrs. Kennedy, on the spur of the moment, doing the interpreting. I couldn't understand what she was saying, but it clearly was not just small talk. She was very knowledgeable about French politics, art, history, and culture, and you could tell by the reaction of her French hosts that they were captivated and impressed.

President Kennedy had to rely on translators, while Mrs. Kennedy could speak directly with her hosts. Nicole Alphand, Mrs. de Gaulle, President Kennedy, President de Gaulle, Mrs. Kennedy, and an unknown woman on arrival in Paris.

Left: It was clear that Mrs. de Gaulle enjoyed being able to converse with Mrs. Kennedy in French, and as she led her by the arm, I walked behind, not understanding a word that was being said.

Opposite: President de Gaulle spent much more time talking with Mrs. Kennedy than with President Kennedy, not only because they could communicate easily in French but because he was mesmerized by her.

She literally beamed with delight as she interacted with the Parisians. Wherever we went, they screamed with admiration and respect. *"OUI!! Vive Jac-qui! Vive Jac-qui!"* Her eyes sparkling, Mrs. Kennedy would wave a gloved hand in acknowledgment, repeating *"Merci, merci,"* over and over. When a crowd broke through a police line and a French reporter stuck a microphone in front of her, she politely responded to their questions for several minutes. This was something she had never done in the States. Mrs. Kennedy viewed this trip not as political but as an international event benefiting both countries. And on a personal level it was, in many ways, a homecoming. She had lived in Paris with a French family while studying at the Sorbonne during her college years and had returned the summer of 1951, when she was twenty-two, with her sister Lee. Now, just ten years later, the city for which she had so much affection had fallen head over heels in love with her too.

Opposite: Coming out of the Hotel de Ville, Jacqueline Kennedy greets the press with a smile. She loved the pageantry of the bands and parades staged by the Parisians.

Left: Mrs. Kennedy rarely spoke to the press at home, but in Paris, she happily answered reporters' questions in French.

There was a lavish dinner each evening, and while all the guests clamored to get close to the American guests of honor, President de Gaulle seemed absolutely transfixed by Mrs. Kennedy, often cornering her in conversation.

Left: President de Gaulle was captivated by Mrs. Kennedy's beauty, charm, and knowledge of French history.

Opposite: President Kennedy beams with pride as he and Mrs. Kennedy depart the Élysée Palace after a dinner in their honor. No one could take their eyes off her.

Mrs. Kennedy had chosen her attire with great care, knowing that all eyes would be on her. She looked absolutely regal and seemed completely at ease as President de Gaulle escorted her through the corridors of Versailles. Mrs. de Gaulle walks behind with an interpreter and President Kennedy (obscured from view).

Top: The dinner in the Hall of Mirrors at Versailles left a great impression on Mrs. Kennedy. An interpreter sits between President Kennedy and President de Gaulle, while Mrs. Kennedy speaks in French with Prime Minister Michel Debré.

Bottom: President de Gaulle and Mrs. Kennedy are engrossed in conversation prior to the playing of the French and American national anthems at the Louis XV theater at Versailles. Madame de Gaulle and President Kennedy are at left.

The highlight of the three-day visit was a white-tie candlelight dinner at Versailles in the Hall of Mirrors, followed by a ballet performance.

President and Mrs. Kennedy were the epitome of glamour as they stepped out of the car and walked up the steps at the entrance of Versailles. But there was also a sense of wonder and delight in their eyes, like they could hardly believe all of this was being done in their honor. Throughout the evening, it was interesting to watch as both men and women kept one eye on her in an effort to seize any opportunity for a moment of polite conversation. Mrs. Kennedy had a permanent smile on her face all evening as she moved effortlessly between French and English, soaking in the magical surroundings, without any hint of realization that she was, without a doubt, the center of all attention. President de Gaulle barely took his eyes off her the entire night, and no one was prouder than her husband.

One of Mrs. Kennedy's friends, Nicole Alphand, was the wife of France's ambassador to the United States, Hervé Alphand. Nicole had offered to arrange anything Mrs. Kennedy wanted to do during the brief visit to Paris, but Mrs. Kennedy had just one request: She wanted to meet André Malraux. Malraux was de Gaulle's minister of culture, but it was his background as an art historian, World War II hero, and novelist that intrigued Mrs. Kennedy. She had read his books in French and shared his belief that the arts were important influential forces on society and culture.

Tragically, Malraux's two sons were killed in an automobile crash just a few days prior to the Kennedys' arrival in Paris. Mrs. Kennedy immediately sent her condolences and made it clear that she certainly didn't expect Malraux to attend any of the functions that had been arranged. But despite his profound and sudden loss, Malraux insisted on keeping his commitments, which included a private luncheon with Mrs. Kennedy the day after the Versailles dinner, at Château de Malmaison, a home that had been restored by Napoleon's Empress Joséphine.

A last-minute addition to the schedule was made when Malraux offered to take Mrs. Kennedy on a private tour of the Impressionist paintings at the Musée du Jeu de Paume prior to the luncheon. Malraux arranged to close the museum temporarily to the public, which left a crowd of somewhat irritated tourists waiting outside in the drizzling rain.

That's me at right in the trench coat, as Mrs. Kennedy and André Malraux arrive at the Musée du Jeu de Paume.

Agent Jim Jeffries was the lead agent on the First Lady's Detail at that time, so he accompanied her in the Citroën bubbletop. I was waiting outside the front entrance of the museum when Mrs. Kennedy arrived with Mr. Malraux. As she exited the car, she appeared somewhat unsure of where to go or how to proceed, and Malraux seemed to sense that. He immediately came to her side and suggested she pose for a few photographs for the tourists who had been told the opening of the museum would be delayed due to their impromptu visit. Malraux beamed, obviously delighted and proud to be able to share the visiting American first lady with the general public, as she smiled graciously for the cameras of the surprised museumgoers. He was a perfect gentleman but also undeniably enamored of her.

Inside the museum, they walked leisurely through the gallery of works by Degas, Renoir, Monet, Manet, and Seurat. I kept a reasonable distance away, but I remember them standing for quite some time in front of a large painting of a nude woman reclining on a sofa or bed. I couldn't understand what they were saying because they were conversing entirely in French, but it was clear that they were enjoying each other's company and on the verge of flirting. There was definitely admiration on both sides. I think that for her, it was intellectually stimulating to be speaking in French with someone who was as interested in art and culture as she was, and he was undoubtedly impressed with her vast knowledge and appreciation of the French masters.

I could tell Mrs. Kennedy would have liked to have stayed much longer touring the exhibits with Malraux, but there was a schedule that had to be kept.

Word had spread that Mrs. Kennedy was in the museum, and the crowd had grown substantially during the hour she was inside. As she headed for the door of the car, a French radio reporter lunged past the police, shoved a microphone toward her, and started rattling off questions in French.

Agent Jeffries put out his arms to keep the reporter away from Mrs. Kennedy, but she calmly intervened and said, "Perhaps I had better talk to the journalists."

She walked past the car and directly into the crowd, clearly inviting them to fire away with questions. It was surprising to me because I'd never seen her

Agent Jim Jeffries (behind Mrs. Kennedy) tries to clear space for Mrs. Kennedy as she speaks to French reporters. You can see the glass-top Citroën the French made especially for her visit so the Parisians could see her from all sides and above.

do anything like this before in Washington. She was always requesting me to keep the press away. But here in Paris, I think she was so eager to make a good impression for the sake of her husband and the fact that she was representing the United States, that she wanted to appear as accessible as possible.

When she was asked, "How did you like the museum?" she replied with all sincerity, "I have just seen the most beautiful paintings in the world. It was a great privilege for me to visit it and especially to have Mr. Malraux conduct me."

"What was your favorite painting?"

Without hesitation, she answered, "I'd have to say it was Manet's *Olympia*," referring to the reclining nude.

What she took away from this short visit to Paris had a tremendous influence on her and how she saw her role as first lady over the next two and a half years. I don't think Mrs. Kennedy fully realized the impact she had made—it wasn't natural for her to focus on her own importance—but over the course of those three dazzling days, I knew I was witnessing the beginning of diplomatic magic.

After Paris, she and André Malraux became sort of pen pals, corresponding regularly, and in May 1962, Malraux and his wife accepted an invitation to the White House.

Mrs. Kennedy took Monsieur and Madame Malraux on a tour of the National Gallery to see some of our country's most celebrated artworks, and, as I recall, this is when she proposed the idea of bringing some of France's masterpieces, like Leonardo da Vinci's *Mona Lisa*, to the United States for a special exhibit.

That evening, May 11, 1962, there was a black-tie dinner at the White House to honor Malraux. Mrs. Kennedy had toiled over the details of this event for weeks. She wanted it to be just perfect. By this point, more than a year into the administration, she had gained a tremendous amount of confidence. She spent the evening at Malraux's side, introducing him to the interesting people she'd invited, whispering in his ear, using all her charms, so that by the end of the evening, he had melted like butter and promised her the *Mona Lisa*.

Mrs. Kennedy and André Malraux had an intellectually flirtatious relationship. On this night at the White House, she convinced him to loan the *Mona Lisa* to the United States.

Alexandria, Virginia, 2019

"So that's the night this photo was taken," Lisa interjected as she held up the dusty framed photograph. "A fond memory and such a special farewell gift with her handwritten dedication to you."

"Yes," I said. "And then, after an immense amount of negotiating and logistical planning, in January 1963, the *Mona Lisa* arrived in Washington, D.C., by ship and under Secret Service protection. It was truly an amazing agreement between our two countries, and it had all been instigated by Mrs. Kennedy. She was really proud of that accomplishment, and President Kennedy was too. It was all due to her ability to connect with both President de Gaulle and André Malraux."

"She was more intelligent than most people thought, wasn't she?" Lisa asked.

"Oh, yes. I think it was during the Paris trip that I realized how educated, well read, and astute she was. I saw her differently after that."

"Well, you had been disappointed when you were given the assignment to be on the First Lady's Detail, right? You felt like it was a demotion after having been with President Eisenhower."

"Absolutely. Up until that point, she hadn't struck me as much different than previous first ladies who stayed in the background. Those first few months after the Inauguration, she was easily fatigued, caring for newborn John and three-year-old Caroline, while at the same time trying to figure out how to create a sense of normal life in the confines of the White House. But everything changed after Paris.

"I gained a new level of respect for her. I saw her authentic curiosity about the treatments being used in a children's hospital; how she moved effortlessly from charming André Malraux, the minister of culture, to mesmerizing President Charles de Gaulle with her deep knowledge of French history; to handling the press with the confidence of a seasoned politician. Almost from the moment she met de Gaulle, his respect for her was unmistakable. Her confidence grew with each interaction and she realized the importance her position could have, as well as the responsibility that came with it.

French minister of culture André Malraux and Mrs. Kennedy pose together next to Leonardo da Vinci's *Mona Lisa* at its unveiling at the National Gallery in Washington, D.C., January 8, 1963.

"It was evident too that President Kennedy was enormously proud of her. He knew she was popular in the United States, but to see her handle that world stage with such grace and confidence, he realized that with her knowledge and language skills, she could be a tremendous asset for the administration's foreign relations agenda. From Paris, they went on to Vienna for the summit with Nikita Khrushchev, premier of the Soviet Union, and even though she didn't speak Russian, Khrushchev was completely beguiled by her. She had a way of really focusing on whomever she was with, and it wasn't an act—she was truly interested in interesting people. She spoke so softly that you had to sort of lean in to hear her, but it made you feel like she didn't want anyone else to be part of this intimate conversation.

"And then, after Vienna, she and the president flew to London for the christening of her sister Lee's daughter, Christina. While they were there, Queen Elizabeth and Prince Philip hosted them at a formal dinner. Think about that: Mrs. Kennedy was thirty-one years old, and the queen of England was just thirty-five."

"Both of them, so young," Lisa said. "At a time when few women were in positions of influence or power. So did you meet Queen Elizabeth?"

"No, I didn't. When they flew to London, I flew directly from Paris to Athens. The prime minister of Greece, Konstantinos Karamanlis, and his wife, Amalia, had extended an invitation to Mrs. Kennedy to visit them. So I headed to Greece to do the advance, while Jim Jeffries—who was the lead agent at that time—accompanied her to London."

"It still amazes me that there were only two Secret Service agents in charge of protecting the first lady back then," Lisa said.

"That's all we had. And because of the complexities of that trip to Paris, she had a new appreciation for what we in the Secret Service did for her and the president. But Agent Jeffries was a lot more rigid than most, and by the time she arrived in Greece, I think she was happy to see me.

In Vienna, Premier Khrushchev was beguiled by Mrs. Kennedy. She spoke so softly that you were compelled to lean in close. She really focused on the person to whom she was speaking.

A wealthy member of Greek parliament named Markos Nomikos provided the use of his villa in the seaside town of Kavouri, along with the use of his 130-foot yacht, *Northwind*, so Mrs. Kennedy could visit some of the Greek islands. Here she is on the island of Hydra accompanied by some Greek authorities and local politicians.

Mrs. Kennedy loved Greece. I was rather conspicuous
in my dark suit and sunglasses, but Mrs. Kennedy
was very relaxed during her 1961 visit following the
intense presidential trip to Paris and Vienna. Flanked
by Mrs. Karamanlis and Prime Minister Karamanlis, she
trusted me to keep the gawking crowds at bay.

Opposite: A special performance of a Greek tragedy was arranged for Mrs. Kennedy and her guests in the 2,400-year-old amphitheater of Epidaurus. Even though it was performed entirely in Greek, she was familiar with the play and absolutely loved it. Sitting next to her on the ancient stone bench is her sister Lee, an unknown woman, and Lee's husband, Prince Stanislas "Stash" Radziwill, and off to the right, that's me, in sunglasses, counting the minutes until it's over.

Left: Mrs. Kennedy loved history, art, and architecture. Greece was, for her, like a living museum where she could imagine walking through the temples during ancient times. Sunset at the Temple of Poseidon was magnificent.

"I had a more relaxed attitude in terms of letting her be spontaneous, but I could also sense when she was feeling uncomfortable in a situation and wanted to make an exit. I learned to read her and anticipate what she wanted. It got so that all she had to do was make eye contact with me and I would take charge of the situation."

"You made her feel safe," Lisa said.

She picked up the framed photo of Mrs. Kennedy and Malraux and looked at me with an impish smile. "Did she ever use those feminine wiles on you? To get you to do things for her?"

"Oh God," I said, shaking my head. "You have no idea."

3

———

THE DIARY

———

ALEXANDRIA, VIRGINIA, 2019

I was sitting at my desk in the basement when Lisa came striding in from the garage.

"Clint, look what I found in a moldy file folder in the trunk."

She was cradling a brown leather book, with a much smaller notebook balanced on top of it, in her purple latex-gloved hands.

"What is it?"

Gingerly grasping the small green booklet between her thumb and forefinger, she handed it to me, and I started to get a sinking feeling.

"It's from 1964," she whispered. "It's your daily diary from 1964."

Engraved in gold lettering on the front, it simply said MEMORANDA. This was the type of little notebook I kept in my coat pocket when I was on the detail. The booklet had clearly come into contact with water, and as I opened it, some of the pages stuck together. Sure enough, that was my handwriting. The ink was smeared in some places but mostly legible.

__Weds__ June 24, 1964
Fog – overcast – cool
Hyannis Port – Boston – NYC
1:30 pm – JBK dep compd in SS-407-X
O'Leary & Hill
431-X fu – Lee

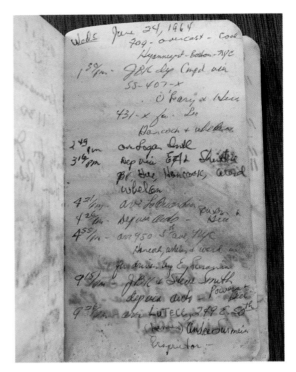

"Wednesday, June 24, 1964," I said aloud as I attempted to decipher the cryptic entry. "I always noted the weather. Fog, overcast, cool. Looks like we were traveling from Hyannis Port to Boston to New York City. One thirty JBK—Jacqueline Bouvier Kennedy—departed the compound in SS-407-X. That was the Secret Service car, a sedan or station wagon we used for her at the Cape. Accompanied by O'Leary and Hill. Muggsy O'Leary had been a driver for JFK when he was a senator and he was sort of an honorary agent. We used him mostly as a driver. Mrs. Kennedy liked him.

"431-X follow-up—Lee. Special Agent Lee was in the follow-up car." I flipped through a few of the fragile pages as a wave of memories crashed into my mind, completely unexpected and without warning.

"I had no idea I still had this," I said. "Don't know why I kept it. I burned all the others."

"Yes, I know," Lisa said. "It kills me every time you mention it. All that history up in flames and turned to ash in your backyard barbecue grill."

"People kept asking me to write books," I said. "I figured if I didn't have any of my notes, they'd stop asking. I had no intention of writing a book." I looked at Lisa and couldn't help but smile. "And then you came along. Talk about using feminine wiles."

Lisa laughed. "I can't deny it," she said. "But you know, Clint, you've never really talked about that year, 1964. You've always just glossed over it and tied it up with a neat little bow."

I didn't know what to say.

"Maybe it's time to deal with it," Lisa prodded.

"Maybe," I said. "We'll see." Eager to change the subject, I nodded toward the other book she was holding. "What's that?"

She held it up so I could see the engraved gold lettering on the spine: THAT PALM BEACH 50.

My long-forgotten 1964 daily diary found in the trunk.

"It's a leather book filled with photos from the fifty-mile hike," she said. "The pictures are amazing."

The front cover was blank but for the small gold print in the lower right-hand corner on the front of it: FOR C. H. FROM M.S.

"For Clint Hill from Mark Shaw," I said. "Mark Shaw was one of Mrs. Kennedy's favorite photographers. She loved his style of documenting events, how he captured candid moments."

I opened the book—it was heavier than I remembered—and flipped through the thick cardstock pages of black-and-white photographs. No words, no text. Just a bunch of photographs telling a crazy story.

"Mrs. Kennedy was pregnant. She had told me, but it wasn't announced in the press until a couple of months later. No one but the participants knew this happened," I said. "It never got out in the press. And then Mark Shaw had these books printed up for us."

I closed the book and looked up at Lisa.

"You asked if Mrs. Kennedy had ever used her feminine wiles on me? Here lies Exhibit A."

4

HYANNIS PORT & PALM BEACH

1963

The extended Kennedy family had a regular annual routine. The summer was spent on Cape Cod, where they had their family compound in Hyannis Port; Labor Day and fall weekends were often spent in Newport, Rhode Island, at Hammersmith Farm, the sprawling estate owned by Mrs. Kennedy's mother and step-father, Janet and Hugh Auchincloss; Thanksgiving was back to Hyannis Port. Christmas, New Year's, and Easter were always in Palm Beach, Florida. The properties were secured by local police along with the agents on the President's Detail who rotated posts around the clock, so the family could really relax without worrying about the press or any outside intruders.

Being in Palm Beach was always a respite from the Washington, D.C., weather and formality of the White House. When the president was there, which was most of the time, they'd go out on the *Honey Fitz* around ten in the morning and not come back until midafternoon. Typically, I'd be on board the yacht along with one of the president's agents, so I witnessed the family and their friends in this close, relaxing environment, and they got used to having the agents around. There was always a lot of activity, with people coming and going, urgent messages being delivered, and conversations and meetings about whatever crises the president was dealing with in a particular moment.

It was a similar environment in Hyannis Port. During the summer, everything centered around the water. Lunchtime cruises on one of the motor yachts, sailing on the *Manitou* or the president's smaller sailboat *Victura*, swimming, and waterskiing. We were always transporting kids and dogs to and from the yachts. Having grown up in North Dakota, in a quiet household with just my sister, Janice, and our parents, to be around this large, vivacious family who loved being together and thrived on constant activity was something entirely new to me. You couldn't help but be swept up in the whirlwind.

Because I was just one of two agents with Mrs. Kennedy—and eventually the only one—I was a permanent fixture. The whole family knew me by name.

There was invariably some kind of competition going on, and because I was always around, I usually got roped into whatever activity was taking place, whether it was waterskiing, touch football, tennis, or a wager around a fifty-mile hike.

February 21, 1963. It was about eight o'clock in the evening and I was off duty. Sitting in my room at Woody's Motel in Palm Beach when the phone rang. I can still hear her voice.

"Oh, Mr. Hill . . ."

"Yes, Mrs. Kennedy?"

"There's something the president and I would like you to do for us . . ."

She knew I wouldn't say no to her, especially when she included the president in the request. It turned out President Kennedy had made a wager with his old friend Chuck Spalding and his brother-in-law Stash Radziwill that they could not complete a fifty-mile hike. Unbeknownst to me, this had been in the works for weeks. Chuck and Stash had hiking boots and had been training. I got roped into it because the president and Mrs. Kennedy were going to go out and check on them periodically, and rather than have a whole bunch of agents and cars—which would alert the press—she figured if I was there, they would be safe.

It was all off the record. All in good fun for them. And a lot of pain for me. The only shoes I had with me were my Florsheim dress shoes. They were sturdy enough, but they weren't made for that. I had blisters for weeks.

Top: In Hyannis Port, the agents blended into the family. There was constant activity, usually revolving around the water, transporting kids and dogs between boats and shore. Here I am with John in 1963.

Bottom: Mrs. Kennedy, Chuck Spalding, Lee Radziwill, me, and Stash Radziwill walking along the Sunshine Highway. Mrs. Kennedy and Lee walked with us for a while, but Chuck, Stash, and I walked the entire fifty miles as part of a wager they had made with President Kennedy. All I got out of the deal were painful blisters from walking in my Florsheim dress shoes.

After completing the fifty-mile hike, President Kennedy placed a construction-paper medal (homemade by Mrs. Kennedy and signed by JFK) around my neck. Left to right: Lee Radziwill, Dr. Max Jacobson, me, President Kennedy, and Stash Radziwill in Palm Beach, February 23, 1963. That silly paper medal is one of my prized possessions.

It took us around twenty hours, including a few stops for rest and to eat. And when we returned back to the house in Palm Beach, they had a little party. Mrs. Kennedy had made these fake medals out of construction paper.

Mine was personalized with my Secret Service code name. It said:

FOR DAZZLE
February 23, 1963
The Order of the Pace Maker
He whom the Secret Service will follow into
the Battle of the Sunshine Highway

President Kennedy had signed it, and then he made a little speech and placed it around my neck.

Alexandria, Virginia, 2019

"I did save that paper medal President Kennedy gave me, you know. *That* medal—now that's something special. One of a kind," I said.

"Yes, thank God," Lisa said. "That is priceless. But can you imagine if you had let some junk dealer take that trunk and go through it? Who knows where this beautiful leather album would have ended up? And look," she said, handing me a piece of fabric she had draped over her arm. "I found this big silk scarf tucked in with some random boxes of yet more presidential cuff links in the trunk. Do you recall the significance of it?"

I unfolded the scarf and laid it across my desk. A black floral pattern was imprinted on the dark purple silk, with delicate burgundy fringe adorning each end. As I inspected it, I noticed something unusual along the edge. A signature.

With Love
from J Ken Galbraith

"John Kenneth Galbraith," I said. "I completely forgot about this."

"The ambassador to India gave you a scarf . . . with love?"

"No, not directly. It was Mrs. Kennedy's. It's a long story."

Lisa stepped behind me, wrapped her arms across my chest, leaned down, and whispered in my ear, "I've got all the time in the world, Mr. Hill."

5

A HISTORIC
JOURNEY

ROME, INDIA, PAKISTAN, LONDON
1962

In September 1961, John Kenneth Galbraith, the Harvard economist appointed by JFK to be the U.S. ambassador to India, had a meeting with President Kennedy in which he suggested the idea of Mrs. Kennedy visiting India. At the time, the administration was delicately juggling maintaining good relations with India while simultaneously providing military aid to its ancient enemy Pakistan, which, Galbraith argued, was a touchy issue. Galbraith suggested that a visit by the first lady would help appease the Indian government by elevating their status.

President Kennedy applauded the idea, and when they approached Mrs. Kennedy, she was enchanted. Galbraith shared Mrs. Kennedy's appreciation for art and tempted her with the things she would see: the Taj Mahal, of course, which deserved two visits—one in the daytime and one by moonlight—but also sites less familiar to Americans like the Sun Temple at Konarak.

I remember her being particularly intrigued by Konarak. Galbraith had told her it was possibly the most wonderful thing in Asia and, as he put it, "exuberantly pornographic." From that moment on, Mrs. Kennedy devoured every book she could find on Indian history and art, and after she learned that I'd been to India just a couple of years earlier with President Eisenhower, she was constantly peppering me with questions.

"What were your impressions of India, Mr. Hill?"

"Dusty. Poor air quality. A thick haze hangs over the cities and there is an ever-present stench. They burn elephant dung for fuel. So, you can imagine, it doesn't smell very nice."

Her eyes widened and I could see her enthusiasm for the trip sinking with every word I uttered. Perhaps Ambassador Galbraith had neglected to mention these things during their discussions of her visit.

"But the people were very nice," I added. "Cooperative, friendly. They were very enthusiastic about Americans visiting their country. But it is extremely densely populated, with many people living in the lower level of the caste system."

"I do want to see how the real people live," she said. "Not just visit the palaces and temples. I told Ambassador Galbraith I want to spend one night in a village."

"One thing you'll see everywhere, no matter where you go, are bicycles," I told her. "Bicycles carrying three, four, even five people. Bicycles, cars, and animals all in the street together. They use camels and oxen like we use trucks—hauling things, pulling wagons. The streets are pure chaos, but somehow they make it work."

Her eyes lit up again with the mention of animals in the streets.

"It's so interesting to see how other cultures live," she said. "I've been reading all about the Mughal emperor Shah Jahan and how he commissioned the Taj Mahal to be built as a mausoleum to honor his wife—his third wife—who died during childbirth. She was the love of his life. Did you visit the Taj Mahal?"

"I did indeed. It's magnificent. Intricate mosaics on the ceilings, walls, and floors. It's a work of art. When our guide told us the story of why it was built, I remember thinking, *Damn, she must have been one hell of a woman.*"

"Oh, Mr. Hill!" She laughed. "I can hardly wait to see it for myself."

The trip was originally supposed to have taken place in November 1961, but it kept getting delayed. At some point during the planning of the India trip, a tour of Pakistan was added.

In July 1961, President Ayub Khan had visited the United States with his daughter Begum Nasir Akhtar Aurangzeb. It was shortly after the Kennedys' trip to Paris, where Mrs. Kennedy had been so impressed with the grand dinner at Versailles, that she came up with the idea to host something similar for her Pakistani guests—a state dinner at Mount Vernon on the banks of the Potomac. She had pulled out all the stops, employing boats as transportation,

President Kennedy, Begum Nasir Akhtar Aurangzeb, Mrs. Kennedy, and Mohammad Ayub Khan at the state dinner in honor of the Pakistani president at Mount Vernon. Mrs. Kennedy and President Ayub Khan bonded over their love of horses and history. When the trip to India was arranged, Mrs. Kennedy was adamant, despite the ancient animosity between India and Pakistan, that she visit both countries.

fife and drum corps as entertainment, and food par excellence by White House chef René Verdon. It was a spectacular event that enhanced the relations between Pakistan and the United States, while causing other subcontinent nations to pay attention. On a personal level, Mrs. Kennedy and President Ayub Khan bonded over their mutual love for horses and riding, and Mrs. Kennedy was enthralled with the charming president's captivating stories of life in Pakistan. He had extended an open invitation to her to visit him in turn.

United States policy toward India and Pakistan was a delicate balancing act because of the ancient rivalry between the two countries and the ongoing dispute over the Kashmir region. But, if Mrs. Kennedy had visited India and not neighboring Pakistan, it would have been a slap in the face to Ayub Khan, who was not only a new American ally but had also become a personal friend.

At the time, Jim Jeffries was still the Special Agent in Charge (SAIC) of the First Lady's Detail, and I was the number-two man. I was assigned to do the advance planning for this historic trip—the first time an American first lady had ever visited India or Pakistan—and it was an ambitious schedule that included a brief stopover in Rome, nearly two weeks traveling all over India, another five days in Pakistan, and a stop in London on the return to Washington. In order to protect her adequately, I was given carte blanche to select a team of agents from the President's Detail and field offices around the country to assist Jeffries and me. Having learned from my previous experience that there was a high probability some of the guys would get sick, I picked seven teams of two men each, with the intention that if one team member was incapacitated, the other could take over.

It had been arranged for Mrs. Kennedy to meet with Pope John XXIII at the Vatican during her thirty-three-hour stopover in Rome. This was yet another historic event, which had tremendous global interest because President Kennedy was the first Catholic U.S. president and Mrs. Kennedy, also a practicing Catholic, would be the first American first lady to have a private audience with the pope. Mrs. Kennedy knew the eyes of the world would be on her, and so did I. It was impossible for me to handle the complex advance arrangements in India, Pakistan, *and* Rome, so I selected Agent Ron Pontius to handle the Rome portion of the trip.

Ron and I had come into the Secret Service on the same day, September 22, 1958, and we had traveled extensively on President Eisenhower's detail together, so I knew him well and knew he had the experience for such an important role. Originally from Chicago, Ron had grown up in a strict Catholic family, and for him to be working directly with the Vatican was one of those once-in-a-lifetime opportunities I knew he'd appreciate. As it turned out, the man in charge of the pope's security at the Vatican, Father Paul Marcinkus, also happened to be from Chicago—and that hometown connection proved to be invaluable.

On February 16, 1962, our team of agents boarded a Pan Am flight from New York's Idlewild Airport to London. Twelve agents and I flew on to New Delhi to set up the complex logistics and security for Mrs. Kennedy's arrival a few weeks later, while Ron Pontius and his partner headed directly to Rome.

6

MRS. KENNEDY
MEETS THE POPE

MARCH 1962

Agent Pontius kept me informed of how everything was going on the first leg of Mrs. Kennedy's trip. All of Rome was abuzz when she arrived on Saturday, March 10. More than a thousand people were waiting in the rain at Leonardo da Vinci Airport to greet her when her plane landed. The Italian government was so concerned about making sure everything was perfect for the first lady's visit that Fiat created a special limousine for her use. And while her sister Princess Lee Radziwill, who was accompanying her on the journey, had the royal title, the Italian press crowned Mrs. Kennedy "America's queen."

After a dinner the first night with friends, Mrs. Kennedy's main event Sunday morning was a rare private audience with Pope John XXIII. Because Lee had been divorced prior to marrying her current husband, Prince Stanislas Radziwill, she was not allowed to attend, but Mrs. Kennedy's loyal maid, Providencia Paredes, who was originally from the Dominican Republic and a devout Catholic, was included in the small entourage of about ten people who were on the list for this extraordinary visit.

A crowd of fifteen thousand people stood in the drizzling rain, waving and cheering, as Mrs. Kennedy entered Vatican City in the official Fiat limousine led by an Italian police motorcycle escort.

Jacqueline Kennedy was the first American first lady to have a private audience with the pope. Posing in the pontiff's private library in the Vatican, March 11, 1962, left to right: Monsignor Pio Benincasa, Mrs. Kennedy, Pope John XXIII, Monsignor Paul Marcinkus (rear), and American archbishop Martin J. O'Connor.

"It was incredible to be there," Pontius told me. He explained minute by minute what happened. How Mrs. Kennedy, guided by a group of archbishops, walked somberly through a maze of marbled hallways that had welcomed kings and queens, princes and princesses, and heads of state—but never, until this moment, the wife of the president of the United States. A row of stern-faced Swiss Guards lined the entryway to the door that opened into the library, a clear sign that the pope was waiting inside.

It had been decided that they would converse in French, which both spoke fluently, but the pope didn't know whether he should address Mrs. Kennedy as "Madame" in French or "Mrs. Kennedy."

"It was so funny, though," Ron recalled. "We walk in and there he is, eighty years old, in his white cassock and red shoes with this beautiful gold braiding. She's supposed to curtsy three times as she walks in, that's the protocol. So she does one curtsy, then she's halfway through the second, and he rushes toward her, breaks into a great big smile, and says, 'Ah, Jacqueline!' It was so spontaneous, like he was her doting grandfather, and it instantly put her at ease as she knelt to kiss his ring."

Pope John inquired about Mrs. Kennedy's children and commented that he had the same name as her husband and son. They exchanged gifts: He gave Mrs. Kennedy Vatican medallions and coins; rosaries for herself, the president, and their two children; and two leather-bound copies of speeches he had made during his pontificate. She had brought him a leather-bound edition of *To Turn the Tide*, a collection of President Kennedy's speeches, which JFK had personally inscribed.

Monsignor Marcinkus instructed the group to stand in a loose semicircle as Pope John walked around and greeted each person, one by one.

"It was so different from the traditional receiving line, in which the president or head of state stands in place as the guests walk by and shake hands," Agent Pontius told me. "You know, you always have those people who want to linger and tell some story or something," he said. "The way the pope did it, with the guests standing stationary in a U-shape, he was able to control the tempo as he walked around, offering a nod and blessing, and then continuing to the next person.

"I was on the end, and when the pope got to me," Pontius continued, "Monsignor Marcinkus said, 'Holy Father, this is Secret Service Agent Ron Pontius. He is one of President Kennedy's senior protective agents and was selected specially to protect Mrs. Kennedy during her stay in Rome.'

"The pope smiled at me and then, in English, he said, 'God bless you, young man. May God bless you in your work.'

"I gotta tell you, Clint. I'm not easily impressed. But for this kid from the South Side of Chicago, that was one of the most incredible moments of my life. The pope speaking directly to me, in English. It was really something."

Provi, Mrs. Kennedy's maid, had a similar reaction. When I saw her in New Delhi, she was still in a state of exhilaration. She could hardly wait to tell me about it.

"I met the pope, Mr. Hill!" she exclaimed. "He knew my name, and he spoke to me in Spanish."

"That's wonderful, Provi," I said. "That is certainly an opportunity few people are lucky enough to have."

"He even shook my hand," she said. "I never can imagine, a poor girl like me from the Dominican Republic, could ever meet the pope."

And while Agent Pontius and Provi had this life-changing semiprivate audience, Mrs. Kennedy was the only one to whom the pope offered a truly private audience.

Pope John accompanied Mrs. Kennedy through three chambers to the Sala Tronetta—the "Little Throne Room"—and for the next thirty-two minutes, Pope John XXIII and Jacqueline Bouvier Kennedy were alone, in what was one of the longest private audiences this pope had ever granted. The next day, the newspapers noted it was six minutes longer than the time he'd spent with Britain's Queen Elizabeth II the previous May.

At some point later, I made some remark, teasing Mrs. Kennedy about how she had upstaged the queen with her visit to the pope.

"Oh, Mr. Hill," she said, "I could have stayed with him for hours. The time flew by. It was all so simple and natural. We didn't talk of anything serious, but just to have that opportunity to be in the presence of His Holiness. With someone who understands the world of men and the world of God. I only wish Jack had been there with me. And the children. I do so hope that someday we'll all be able to go back together."

She was used to getting special treatment because her husband was the president of the United States, and usually some kind of political favor was expected in return, but on this occasion, there was no quid pro quo. I had accompanied her to Mass so many times, witnessed her taking Communion, and watched as she prayed. Her faith was strong, and there was no doubt Mrs. Kennedy's private audience with the pope had been a moving experience for her.

Meanwhile, the schedule had been changed countless times and many of the agents had indeed gotten sick and were sidelined due to the unpleasant and physically debilitating effects of the unfamiliar foods and tainted water in the weeks leading up to Mrs. Kennedy's arrival in India. I'd lost at least six pounds, and there were other guys who were down twenty. We had no medic or doctor to call to provide medication, so everyone was on their own when it came to dealing with the gastrointestinal issues we were all having. A few guys who'd had the foresight to bring some Kaopectate with them had to guard it like it was gold. My biggest concern was making sure Mrs. Kennedy didn't get sick.

I was meeting with Ambassador Galbraith daily, and on one occasion he was composing a letter to Mrs. Kennedy. Because of all the delays, I could tell he was somewhat worried—and not without reason—that she might cancel the trip altogether.

"I want her to know how much this means to the people of India," he said. "The interest in her visit promises to be rather greater than that of the recent appearance of the queen of England."

"Yes, Ambassador," I said, "but our concern—and the president's concern—is that the schedule will be exhausting for her. You don't want to be embarrassed when you have to cancel something because, trust me, she will have no qualms about skipping a morning meet-and-greet with local dignitaries if she's been up too late the night before."

Galbraith promised there would be no engagements of any kind before ten o'clock in the morning, no more than two serious events a day, and, on some days, she'd be able to sleep until noon. After initially seducing Mrs. Kennedy with the risqué nature of the temple of Konarak, it was decided that the temptation of the press to photograph the first lady in front of sexually explicit carvings might not be in the best interest of either country and ultimately it was dropped from the itinerary.

7

INDIA

MARCH 1962

Ambassador Galbraith had flown to Rome so he could accompany Mrs. Kennedy and Lee on the flight from Rome to New Delhi. By the time Mrs. Kennedy and Lee arrived in India on March 12, the anticipation in the country had built to the point that it felt like a dam was about to burst. I was pacing the tarmac at Palam Airport as the Air India jet landed, eager and somewhat anxious about how Mrs. Kennedy was going to react to the ambitious schedule set forth for the first day. The crowds were much larger than we had anticipated. Thousands had come to greet her at the airport, and with all the women in their brightly colored saris—every shade of pink, purple, orange, yellow, and blue you can imagine—the sea of people looked like a paint palette. The sheer number of people was astonishing to me. This was not the president; it was the first lady. Galbraith had told me there'd be tremendous interest in her visit here, but it wasn't until I saw it with my own eyes that I realized the vastness of her popularity.

The crowd cheered when the door near the cockpit opened, and as Mrs. Kennedy emerged from the plane, she smiled with delight at the sight of some familiar faces.

Top: Ambassador J. Kenneth Galbraith, Indira Gandhi, Kitty Galbraith, Mrs. Kennedy, and Jawaharlal Nehru in the gardens at the prime minister's residence. Each afternoon, Nehru walked with Mrs. Kennedy and her sister Lee through the gardens for exercise and conversation.

Bottom: Mrs. Kennedy turns to look at the press bus as she gets into the waiting Mercedes convertible with Indira Gandhi outside the palace. Agent Jim Jeffries is standing at the left front of the car, while I'm up ahead on the right, giving instructions to the motorcycle escort.

Prime Minister Jawaharlal Nehru and his daughter, Indira Gandhi, who had been honored with a state dinner at the White House the previous November, were waiting at the bottom of the steps to greet her, along with the Indian ambassador to the United States, Braj Kumar Nehru, and an array of other government officials. Someone immediately approached her with an enormous garland of flowers, and she bowed her head so it could be placed around her neck, obviously having been briefed on this arrival ritual. Lee would always remain several paces behind; she knew her sister was the star, and she was just lucky to be able to share this adventure with her.

I could tell Mrs. Kennedy was truly excited to finally be here after so many months of preparations and delays, but there was a sense of apprehension too. A lot was riding on this visit, diplomatically and politically. She was just thirty-two years old, but she was far savvier than most people realized. The mere fact that President Kennedy had encouraged this solo trip was a testament to his faith in her ability to strengthen the bond between our two nations.

Thousands of local residents—men, women, children of all ages, snake charmers, and people atop camels—stood along the roadway waving and cheering as Mrs. Kennedy rode by in an open Mercedes convertible, sitting in the back seat next to Indira Gandhi, on the way to the ambassador's guesthouse at the U.S. Embassy.

As it turned out, President Rajendra Prasad had just addressed Parliament and there was a grand parade about to take place as he returned to Rashtrapati Bhavan, the presidential mansion. Mrs. Kennedy was scheduled to meet with President Prasad later, but Prime Minister Nehru suggested she might also like to view the parade prior to their meeting.

"Oh, I'd love to!" Mrs. Kennedy said. It wasn't on the schedule, and Agent Jeffries tried to dissuade her from this impromptu change within the first hours of the visit. It wasn't typical of me to override a supervisor, but I knew this pageantry was just the kind of thing Mrs. Kennedy loved.

"Let her do it, Jim," I urged. "We'll get her in a safe place and make sure she's covered."

She watched from a viewing platform as row after row of horse-mounted bodyguards in bright red tunics and fancy turbans marched past, escorting the seventy-seven-year-old president in his own horse-drawn carriage. As Prime Minister Nehru explained the meaning of the various costumes, Mrs. Kennedy had a constant smile on her face, commenting on the beauty of the horses and the way the choreography paid tribute to India's heritage.

"It's wonderful to see how you've preserved your history and civilization with this tradition," she said. "I think it's so important for every country to find ways to remember its past and to keep history alive. Thank you so much for suggesting this, Prime Minister."

Right: An army of press surrounded Mrs. Kennedy throughout the India visit. "Follow me," I told her. I'd lead the way while one of the other agents would be next to her or behind.

Opposite:
Mrs. Kennedy was moved by her visit to Gandhi's memorial site. The tall man at left is Ambassador J. Kenneth Galbraith. He and Mrs. Kennedy had a wonderful friendship, and both had a deep appreciation for history, the arts, and architecture. Her visit played an enormous role in strengthening relations between our two countries.

She had a brief meeting with Prasad, and then our entire entourage headed to Old Delhi to the tomb of Mohandas K. Gandhi. There was an army of press, Indian security officials, and a growing number of locals who were crowding around Mrs. Kennedy.

"Stay close to Ambassador Galbraith and follow me, Mrs. Kennedy," I instructed. Our small team of Secret Service agents formed a strategic circle around her and her hosts, supplemented by Indian security officials, so we were close enough to act if needed but not so close as to make her feel we were hovering. I had learned that, in these types of situations, it made her feel comfortable seeing me ahead of her, knowing that I'd lead her in the appropriate direction.

"Let me worry about your security and the logistics," I'd told her many times. "That's my job. I won't let anything happen to you."

As we walked, she listened intently as she was given a brief history lesson in Gandhi's importance to the people of India and its independence—history she already knew, of course—and why he was revered as the unofficial "Father of India." There was a moment of silent reflection as she somberly laid a wreath of white roses on Gandhi's simple tomb, the place where he was cremated, after being assassinated fourteen years earlier by a Hindu nationalist firing three bullets into his chest.

I was with Mrs. Kennedy for the first three days in New Delhi, and everything was going smoothly. There were opulent luncheons and dinners in her honor, but what she enjoyed most was experiencing the arts, culture, and traditions of these people and this land that was so vastly different from America and Europe. The biggest problem we had was that everyone wanted to be near her. In the Hindu religion, it is believed that if you can get close to or touch someone who is famous or greatly admired, their good karma rubs off on you. But I was worried about the opposite happening.

The welfare of children, especially children who were hospitalized, was very important to her. I think it might have come from stories President Kennedy had shared with her about his boyhood illnesses, when he was bedridden for lengthy periods. She had genuine empathy for the loneliness of the children who couldn't be outside playing or going to school with the others. Every place we went, there was typically a visit to a children's hospital, where she'd get a briefing on the kinds of treatments they were using and then she'd go around and talk to the kids, offering lollipops or some other treats.

Mrs. Kennedy had expressed a desire to experience how the locals lived and shopped, but we had come to the conclusion that it would be better to arrange for her to shop in controlled environments. At a tour of the Central Cottage Industries Emporium in New Delhi, she spoke with artists and craftsmen and was treated to a fashion show of Indian and Western-style clothing in which Ambassador Galbraith's wife, Kitty, made a surprise appearance as one of the models. She was presented with jewelry, pottery, and all kinds of sketches and paintings, but before purchasing anything, she queried the price, which was always in Indian rupees.

"And how much is that in dollars?" she'd ask the ambassador. He'd do the math, and, once she made her decision, he'd pull out a wad of bills and pay the vendor. Mrs. Kennedy never carried any money. Usually I was the one doling out cash for her spur-of-the-moment purchases, but in India the ambassador took care of everything and presumably submitted the receipts to the State Department for reimbursement from the Kennedys' personal account.

The people of India were so excited to see Mrs. Kennedy, and they would close in around us as they clamored to touch her. That's me, plowing through the crowd, in New Delhi, with Mrs. Kennedy in the hat, turning to smile at the people, many of whom brought their children for this once-in-a-lifetime experience of seeing the first lady from America.

Above: Mrs. Kennedy hands out lollipops to delighted
children in a hospital in India. Everywhere we went,
throughout the world, she always made a point to visit
local children's hospitals. She was interested in different
treatments used in different countries, but, more important,
she wanted to bring a bit of joy to children who couldn't
play outside or go to school.

Opposite: Indira Gandhi (left) and Mrs. Kennedy watch
pottery being made as Agent Paul Rundle and I stand
back and observe. Because of the tremendous crowds,
we had to arrange for Mrs. Kennedy to shop in controlled
environments.

Right: When Air India presented Mrs. Kennedy with a gift of two tiger cubs, she had visions of them roaming the White House lawn. Prime Minister Nehru is pointing to the cubs as Mrs. Kennedy looks at them with delight. Her sister Lee is at right with Ambassador Galbraith in the plaid jacket standing behind her.

Opposite: Mrs. Kennedy loved animals. She had no fear. Here she's feeding a baby elephant from a bottle, and as it wraps its trunk around her arm, she bursts into laughter.

On top of the mementos and souvenirs Mrs. Kennedy bought for herself, family, and friends, everywhere we went she was presented with gifts from her hosts. Someone at the State Department was responsible for keeping track and making sure everything made its way back to Washington. But some of the gifts created problems—like the two tiger cubs presented to her as a farewell gift from Air India. Mrs. Kennedy loved animals of every kind and she had visions of the tigers roaming the White House lawn. Unfortunately for the cubs, they came down with some intestinal problem and died a couple of days later. The nice folks at Air India wanted to replace them, but those of us who knew what a headache it would be trying to get them back to Washington were trying to quash that idea.

Every afternoon, there was time allotted for Mrs. Kennedy to relax. She and Lee would walk around the gardens with Prime Minister Nehru, talking and enjoying a bit of exercise. Mrs. Kennedy enjoyed Nehru's company, and often the prime minister would slip his arm into hers as they were walking. It wasn't romantic, but more a sort of paternal affection.

On one of those first days in New Delhi, Mrs. Kennedy pulled out a little gadget that at first I thought was a lipstick holder or makeup compact. She and Lee were looking at it and giggling like schoolgirls. It wasn't until she held it up to her eye that I realized it was a miniature camera.

"What have you got there, Mrs. Kennedy?" I asked.

"Oh, it's a tiny camera that Mark Shaw gave me before we left," she said, laughing. "I told him I wished I had a camera I could tuck into my purse, and he gave this to me."

"That's very interesting," I said. "May I see it?"

She sidled up next to me and said, "It's really very clever. See, it's closed now, but all you do is slide it like this and it exposes the lens and viewfinder." It said MINOX on one side, and, pointing to three dials on the other side, she explained the very small numerical markings. "This is the ASA film-speed setting. This one is the shutter speed, and this is the focusing range."

She had been a photographer for a newspaper before she married JFK, and she clearly knew what she was doing. I had gone to a special photography school while in the Counter Intelligence Corps prior to joining the Secret Service, so I had some knowledge of cameras and how they functioned too. But she didn't know that.

"How many pictures can you take with each roll of film?" I asked.

"Oh, that's what's so amazing. The rolls of film are about the size of your fingernail, but you can take fifty pictures with each little roll." She looked up at me and, with a sly smile, added, "It's a spy camera."

I held the camera up to my eye and pointed it at her. "I think I'm the one that should have a spy camera."

"Give that back to me, Mr. Hill!" She laughed as she reached for the camera. "You never know, maybe I'll be spying on you."

It was all in good fun, but it also gave me an idea: A camera like that might very well come in handy.

Lee and Mrs. Kennedy trying to figure out how to work the "spy camera" they had been given by photographer friend Mark Shaw. They were a real novelty back in 1962, and I thought it would be beneficial for me to have one too.

During my advance planning negotiations with Ambassador Galbraith, I had suggested it would be a special treat for Mrs. Kennedy if we could arrange for her to have an afternoon set aside for riding somewhere. Galbraith had the ideal solution: the exercise grounds of the elite cavalry regiment of the Indian Army, known as the President's Bodyguard.

It was her third day in Delhi, and after another busy day that included presenting a children's art exhibit to Indira Gandhi as a gift from the United States, Mrs. Kennedy was thrilled to get away from the handshaking and smiling, change into her riding attire of jodhpurs and boots, and climb onto a beautiful horse named Princess. She was giddy with excitement as she rode with Ambassador Galbraith and the elite Indian riders, galloping and jumping around the pristine fields as the sun began to set. This was a private event, with no press allowed, but Galbraith had invited Benno Graziani, an old photographer pal of Mrs. Kennedy's who was on the trip representing *Paris Match*, to take some private pictures.

The vigorous exercise away from the smothering crowds and press was just what she needed. When they were finished riding, Mrs. Kennedy was beaming.

"Oh, Ken, darling," she said. "That was marvelous! Thank you so much for arranging it."

Galbraith looked at me, standing off to the side, and said, "You're so very welcome, Mrs. Kennedy. It was actually Clint who suggested you might need a break around this point. I merely made the phone call."

Mrs. Kennedy looked at me, her eyes bright, her cheeks flushed from the exercise, and laughed. "Mr. Hill certainly does know me well."

Lee, who had come to watch and was in a particularly jovial mood, added, "A Secret Service man is supposed to know all your secrets, Jackie." Then, turning to me, she asked coyly, "Do you know all her secrets, Mr. Hill?"

"They're secrets," I said, trying not to smirk. "I can neither confirm nor deny."

Everyone laughed as they picked up their things and we all piled back into the cars. There was a gala dinner at the prime minister's residence that night, and Mrs. Kennedy couldn't show up in her riding attire.

Mrs. Kennedy using her spy camera to take photos of the press while lounging with Ambassador Galbraith at the ambassador's residence in New Delhi.

Above: Ambassador Galbraith and I arranged for
Mrs. Kennedy to have an afternoon riding with members
of the Indian cavalry regiment, the President's Bodyguard.
She was an excellent horsewoman, and riding gave her
a great deal of pleasure.

Opposite: Mrs. Kennedy was so happy to have an
afternoon of riding during the busy schedule in India.
That's me on the right in my suit and tie, standing by as
Ambassador Galbraith, Mrs. Kennedy, and Lee share a
laugh with a couple of our Indian hosts. It was a privilege
to be part of those joyful moments. When you travel
with someone—particularly in a foreign country—you
experience things that can't be fully appreciated by
anyone who wasn't there.

When I look at that photograph of Mrs. Kennedy so completely relaxed, laughing with her sister and her good friend Ambassador Galbraith, it brings back such fond memories. What a privilege it was to experience those moments with her.

I went on to Pakistan the next morning, leaving her with Agent Jeffries in charge. I had faith in the capable agents who had gone ahead to Agra, Udaipur, and Jaipur, but I detected tension between Mrs. Kennedy and Jeffries. I could only hope that everything would go smoothly.

Top: Mrs. Kennedy was eager to take part in all the Indian customs. Here Prime Minister Nehru adorns Mrs. Kennedy's forehead with color during Holi, a Hindu festival celebrating the arrival of spring.

Bottom: Mrs. Kennedy is presented with garlands of flowers around her neck as she arrives in Jaipur.

Opposite: Mrs. Kennedy loved being immersed in the pageantry and traditions of India.

Opposite: Mrs. Kennedy had read volumes about India's history, and visiting the Taj Mahal both during the day and at night was spectacular.

Left: Mrs. Kennedy and her sister had a lot of fun together. I imagine, by the mischievous look on her face, that they were probably giving the perplexed elephant driver instructions to go somewhere or do something they'd been told not to do.

Right: Mrs. Kennedy had a wonderful sense of adventure. She was eager to try anything—the more exotic the better—and she loved sharing these adventures with her sister Lee. Here they are atop an elephant in the courtyard of the Amber Palace in Jaipur, India.

Mrs. Kennedy was fascinated by the young men, clad only in loincloths, who jumped fifty feet into the water tank at Fatehpur Sikri. "You're so brave!" she said as she reached out to shake the hand of one dripping-wet young man. It was important to her to be able to interact with the common people in India and not just be exposed to the upper echelon.

Above: Mrs. Kennedy stands out in white next to the Indian ladies in their colorful saris at this formal dinner in Udaipur. At left, behind her, is the Indian ambassador to the United States, B. K. Nehru. The maharajah of Udaipur, Lee Radziwill, and Ambassador J. Kenneth Galbraith stand at right.

Left: It was nearly impossible for Mrs. Kennedy to go to local shops because of the massive interest in her visit. Here, prior to a dinner at Raj Bhavan in Jaipur, merchants bring selections of jewelry. Ambassador Galbraith and the daughter of the governor of Rajasthan, Tej Khanna, assist in her selections.

Opposite:
Mrs. Kennedy and Lee shopping for Indian artwork. Even though a visit to the Konarak temple, with its sexually explicit carvings, was scratched from the itinerary, Mrs. Kennedy found some *Kama Sutra* etchings to bring home—which she ultimately hung in the dining room of Wexford, the home she and the president had built near Middleburg, Virginia.

Left: Mrs. Kennedy tried to steal some quiet moments during the busy schedule Ambassador Galbraith had set for her. During a tour of the Lake Palace hotel, on Lake Pichola, she relaxes on the bed in one of the suites with the maharani of Udaipur.

Above: At Lake Pichola in Udaipur, Mrs. Kennedy takes a relaxing boat ride as press photographers are nearly capsized in the overloaded boat that struggles to keep up. Seated next to her are Ambassador B. K. Nehru, the maharani of Udaipur, and Princess Lee Radziwill.

Opposite: Dressed in peach, Mrs. Kennedy turns to smile, giving the press photographers the shot they wanted.

Right: Mrs. Kennedy called her trip to India and Pakistan "magical."

Opposite top: The government laid pathways of carpet over the dirt roads so Mrs. Kennedy's shoes didn't get soiled, and provided someone to shade her with a large umbrella from the blazing-hot sun. As she and Ambassador Galbraith walk down to the boat ramp on the Ganges River, crowds of locals and press try to get as close as possible.

Opposite bottom: Lee, Ambassador Galbraith, and Mrs. Kennedy, in pink, take a boat ride on the Ganges River. Mrs. Kennedy was fascinated by the riverfront steps in Varanasi, called ghats, where the locals bathed, gathered water, and performed cremation ceremonies, all in the same river.

8

––––––

PAKISTAN

––––––

MARCH 1962

I was in Karachi, where the U.S. Embassy was located at that time, setting up all the details for Mrs. Kennedy's impending arrival. One night I was awakened in my hotel room by someone banging on the door, telling me I had an urgent message at the embassy.

As it turned out, there were actually three TOP SECRET communications for me, all with the same message:

```
PROCEED FIRST AVAILABLE FLIGHT TO LAHORE, PAKISTAN.
UPON ARRIVAL OF MRS. KENNEDY IN LAHORE ON
MARCH 21 FROM NEW DELHI, YOU ARE TO ASSUME
COMMAND OF FIRST LADY'S PROTECTIVE DETAIL.
```

I was stunned. Clearly, my instincts about friction with Jeffries were not unfounded. But still, it was a most unusual way to be promoted.

The government had declared the day of Mrs. Kennedy's arrival a holiday, and thousands upon thousands of Pakistani citizens were at the airport and standing along the route into Lahore, waving and cheering. Mrs. Kennedy rode with President Ayub Khan in the back seat of a dark green Oldsmobile convertible, and as we got closer into Lahore, he urged her to stand so the people could see her better. It was an enormous honor and acknowledgment of Pakistan's proud heritage that the American first lady would travel halfway around the world to visit, and to show their gratitude, the people tossed handfuls of flower petals and sometimes even full bouquets at the car as we drove by. Mrs. Kennedy was thrilled with the enthusiastic reception, and it seemed she could hardly believe it. She'd become accustomed to the enormous crowds along motorcades when she traveled with President Kennedy, but in India and now here in Pakistan, the attention was solely for her. I must admit, I too was surprised by the sheer numbers of people and their genuine excitement. I don't recall any first lady, before or since, having been greeted in a foreign country with such massive crowds when the president wasn't with her. It was extraordinary.

Mrs. Kennedy's visit happened to coincide with West Pakistan's National Horse and Cattle Show. It was a huge event, much like a state fair, with people showing their prized bulls and horses, with the added entertainment of dancing camels. After watching the festivities in the stands for a while, President Ayub Khan invited Mrs. Kennedy to join him on the ground level for a closer look at some of the animals. It was a hot day and Mrs. Kennedy had taken off her coat, which I held over my arm as I followed her into the arena. There was a bit of commotion, and then two guards wearing bright red military jackets and turbans emerged with a beautiful sable-colored horse.

"My dear Mrs. Kennedy," Ayub Khan said, "on behalf of the people of Pakistan, I present to you Sardar."

Mrs. Kennedy was thoroughly surprised, as was I. No one had given any indication that she was going to be given a horse as a gift. She was beyond thrilled as she walked up to the horse.

"Oh, aren't you beautiful!" she said as she caressed his nose with her white-gloved hands.

I had suddenly been placed in charge of Mrs. Kennedy's protective detail the day before her arrival in Pakistan. Thousands lined the streets of Lahore to welcome her. She and President Ayub Khan stand in the open car, laughing as people throw flower petals and bouquets.

91

Top: When Ayub Khan presented Mrs. Kennedy with a beautiful horse named Sardar, I was standing behind her, holding her coat, thinking, *How the hell am I going to get that damn horse back to Washington?*

Bottom: Mrs. Kennedy fell in love with Sardar from the moment she saw him.

Beaming with delight at her reaction, President Ayub Khan said, "It is my hope that every time you ride Sardar, you will remember with fondness the time you spent in Pakistan." It was an incredibly generous and thoughtful gift, which showed just how well President Ayub Khan knew Mrs. Kennedy. Nothing could have pleased her more. Giving unique and meaningful gifts to her family and friends was something that was important to Mrs. Kennedy, and for someone to do the same for her was truly special. Of course, all I had running through my mind was the thought *How the hell am I going to get that damn horse back to Washington?*

As Mrs. Kennedy toured Pakistan, everywhere we went, crowds of people lined the streets in the cities and even on the rural roads into the smaller villages, just to see her drive by. I had been in Pakistan in 1959 accompanying President Eisenhower, and one of the things that really stood out was that the crowds were almost exclusively male. It was rare to see a woman out in public, due to the country's strict Muslim customs, and if we did, they were completely covered by the traditional burka. I began to realize that there was something different about the people showing up for Mrs. Kennedy: This time there were many women and girls among the crowds. It was remarkable.

And Mrs. Kennedy did not disappoint. At an evening gala held at the Shalimar Gardens in Lahore—an oasis of flowering plants set amid wandering pools, marble pavilions, and over four hundred fountains designed by the same Mughal ruler who had commissioned the Taj Mahal in India—Mrs. Kennedy surprised me by giving a short speech, completely spur of the moment.

She spoke about how she'd dreamed all her life of visiting these gardens and how she wished her husband could be there to experience it too.

With a steady voice, she appeared entirely at ease in front of the microphone. "I must say I'm profoundly impressed by the reverence which you in Pakistan have for your art and for your culture and for the use that you make of it now. My own countrymen too have a pride in their tradition, so I think that as I stand in these gardens, which were built long before my country was born, that's one more thing that binds us together and that always will. We'll always share an appreciation of the finer things."

In a telegram back to President Kennedy, Ambassador Walter McConaughy wrote that the turnout of people "on streets, at stadium, and at Shalimar Gardens has been largest, friendliest, and most demonstrative of any in recent years. Enthusiastic participation of unusual numbers of women, especially young women, particularly noteworthy."

McConaughy remarked that the governor ascribed this to the "realization by Pakistani women that this notable recognition of one of their own sex is symbolic of the rising status of women here in Pakistan," and that Mrs. Kennedy's speech at the Shalimar Gardens "had an impact well beyond anything a man could have achieved. I believe she has made a singular contribution to our cause in these two days."

It was not an overstatement. Just by being herself and showing her sincere interest in the people of Pakistan, Mrs. Kennedy was more effective than any ambassador or diplomatic relations policy had been before or since in creating goodwill between our two countries. And while she was genuinely interested, kind, and thoughtful, diplomacy was not the issue at the top of her mind.

Shortly before McConaughy relayed the telegram, he asked Mrs. Kennedy, "Is there any message you'd like me to transmit to the president?"

"Yes, there is." Mrs. Kennedy smiled slyly. "Please ask the president to find out if there are any provisions under the quarantine regulations that would allow that magnificent horse to be exempted from going into thirty-day quarantine."

Diplomacy and politics aside, her biggest concern was the health and well-being of the horse. She wasn't convinced that Ambassador McConaughy would get the message across to her husband with as much fervor as was needed, so she composed her own telegram.

It was very late when she called for me to come to her room.

"Oh, Mr. Hill," she said, "would you please send this telegram right away. It's extremely urgent. I just can't bear the thought of Sardar in quarantine for a month. I want to be able to ride him as soon as I get back."

As it turned out, while she was making history, shaping international relations with strategic countries on the other side of the world, President Kennedy was spending the weekend in Palm Springs, California, where he was being entertained at the home of Bing Crosby. So I sent the telegram, labeled SECRET EYES ONLY, to President Kennedy in Palm Springs.

DEAR JACK,

IT SEEMS SO RUDE TO PAKISTANIS TO SUGGEST THAT THEIR
BEAUTIFUL HORSE HAS HOOF AND MOUTH DISEASE WHEN OBVIOUSLY
HE HASN'T A GERM IN THE WORLD.

HE IS SO BEAUTIFUL AND HIGH STRUNG IT WOULD BE CRUEL
TO QUARANTINE HIM IN NEW YORK FOR THIRTY DAYS. CANNOT
BEAR TO BE PARTED FROM HIM THAT LONG AS COULD SHOW
HIM THIS SPRING AND START SCHOOLING HIM IMMEDIATELY.

COULD YOU NOT HAVE VETERINARIAN EXAMINE HIM IN NEW YORK
AND SAY HE WAS FREE FROM ALL DISEASE.

IT WOULD BE LIKE LEAVING LEE IN QUARANTINE TO PART WITH
HIM—ESPECIALLY AS HE HAS BEEN SO FRIGHTENED PAST FEW
DAYS BY PHOTOGRAPHERS.

LOVE JACKIE

I couldn't help but laugh to myself when I read her plea to the president. The question was: Could it be pulled off without creating an international incident or inciting political backlash?

Oⁿe of the most memorable parts of the entire trip was our excursion to the Khyber Pass.

We flew to Peshawar in the northwest region of Pakistan, and the entire entourage of press people, staff, local security officials, a couple of other agents, and even Mrs. Kennedy's personal maid, Provi, all piled into the buses and cars. The local people had come out in droves—hanging out of open windows, cheering from balconies, piled on rooftops—waving and clapping as we wound through the ancient streets of Peshawar, the gateway to the legendary Khyber Pass.

It was a harrowing ride as we climbed higher and higher, around hairpin turns on the centuries-old road etched between cliffs of shale and limestone. Sitting in the front seat between the driver and President Ayub Khan's military aide, I didn't like the fact that I couldn't see what might be coming at us as we rounded one corner after another, but Mrs. Kennedy, who was in the back seat with her sister Lee, thought it was a wonderful adventure.

"Oh, how I wish Jack could experience this," she said. "To be traveling the same route as Alexander the Great and Genghis Khan. He would love it."

I turned to look back at her. Her eyes were wide with the delight of a child on a carnival ride. "Imagine navigating this on horseback or camel, Mr. Hill!" she said.

"Oh, you would love that, I'm sure," I said with a smile. "You would have left me in the dust five miles back."

Our first stop was Jamrud Fort. The press people scrambled out of their bus, and as they jockeyed for position to capture Mrs. Kennedy's every move, I noticed some of them looked rather green.

As Mrs. Kennedy was introduced to the white-bearded chieftains of the frontier tribes, all dressed in traditional tunics with daggers hanging from low-slung leather belts, she greeted each one with a genuine smile and the same respect she would show to President Charles de Gaulle or Queen Elizabeth. They presented her with the gift of a jeweled dagger and then brought out a lamb draped in a colorful scarf. When she reached down and stroked its little head, I cringed. Agent Ron Pontius, who had done the advance for this part of the trip, had warned me that they were actually planning to sacrifice the lamb

Now the Special Agent in Charge, I rode in the middle front seat of the car, with Mrs. Kennedy in the rear. People lined the streets of villages as we passed through, waving and cheering.

in her honor. My mind flashed back to the time I was driving her in the station wagon in Middleburg, Virginia, and came upon a turtle crossing the country road. I couldn't stop in time, and when she heard the *crunch crunch* under the tires, her hands flew to her mouth in shock.

"Oh, Mr. Hill! What have you done!"

I didn't want to even imagine her reaction when one of those nice old men whipped out his dagger and sliced it across the cute little lamb's throat. We hastily changed the schedule so we could get her out of there before the poor animal lost its life.

"Time to go, Mrs. Kennedy," I said as I gently put my hand on the small of her back. "We need to stay on schedule so we can get back before dark."

From that point on, our conspicuous caravan was escorted by members of the Khyber Rifles, the Pakistani Army's paramilitary force responsible for securing the border. We drove several more treacherous miles, up, up, up, around, and around, until we reached Landi Kotal, the headquarters of the Khyber Rifles.

Mrs. Kennedy watched and listened with rapt attention as the uniformed Khyber Rifles troops performed a welcome ceremony with bagpipes and drums. She took in every facet of the music, the uniforms, and the rugged environs so that when she returned home, she could regale her husband with details of this most unusual excursion.

We walked up a wide road to the Khyber Pass, which was clearly marked by a hand-painted sign that said KHYBER PASS. Farther on was a much larger sign that warned:

FRONTIER OF PAKISTAN
TRAVELLERS ARE NOT PERMITTED TO PASS
THIS NOTICE BOARD
UNLESS THEY HAVE COMPLIED WITH
THE PASSPORT REGULATIONS

At Jamrud Fort in Pakistan, the tribal chieftains presented Mrs. Kennedy (accompanied by her sister Lee) with a jeweled dagger and a lamb. As she stroked the lamb's head, she was unaware that they were planning to sacrifice the animal in her honor.

Left: Mrs. Kennedy wearing President Ayub Khan's lambswool karakul cap. When the president bid farewell to Mrs. Kennedy that morning, she commented on how much she liked his cap. He took it off his head and placed it on hers, and she wore it the rest of the day. I would guess that was the first time a Pakistani karakul cap was worn with a Chanel suit.

Right: Mrs. Kennedy was fascinated by the history of the Khyber Pass and the stories of those who had traveled through these strategic mountains.

Top: I stayed close to Mrs. Kennedy as we walked toward the border at the Khyber Pass. From left to right: Ayub Khan's military aide, Mrs. Kennedy, me, and the governor of West Pakistan in the turban.

Bottom: Mrs. Kennedy thought it was amusing when one of the American press photographers ignored the huge sign warning not to step foot into Afghanistan and was hauled back by a member of the Khyber Rifles.

We were walking on a downward sloping path toward the sign when one of the press photographers ran ahead of the group to try to get a particular shot. Just as he was about to step into Afghan territory, one of the Khyber Riflemen raced toward him.

"*Yala! Yala!* No go! No go!"

He grabbed the oblivious photographer's arm and forcefully pulled him backward, nearly toppling him to the ground.

Mrs. Kennedy found it very amusing. She had tolerated the press following her on this trip because it was an official state visit, but, had it been necessary, I doubt she would have intervened on behalf of the errant newsman like she had for Sardar. In her pecking order, the press ranked well below horses.

We had lunch at the Khyber Rifles mess and then it was time to head back to Peshawar. I was talking with Gordon Parks, one of our great White House Communications Agency guys, when Cecil Stoughton, the White House photographer, came up to us and said, "Clint, Gordy. Stand over there by the sign. I'll get your picture."

I usually tried to avoid being in any photographs, but this time I was glad I took him up on the offer. How many people have a photo of themself in front of the Khyber Rifles officers' mess?

Animals had been a recurring theme on this exotic trip. There had been gifts of tigers, a horse, and a lamb; Mrs. Kennedy and Lee had ridden an elephant in Jaipur, India; and on the final day in Pakistan, it was all about a camel. We were back in Karachi, and Mrs. Kennedy had a letter from Vice President Johnson she had promised to deliver to a camel driver named Bashir, whom LBJ had befriended on his trip to Pakistan the year before. It was all set up for the press to be there. One last great photo op of Mrs. Kennedy with the camel driver and his beloved camel.

I should have expected it, but Mrs. Kennedy took me by surprise when, after handing Bashir the letter, she asked him if she and Lee could ride the camel. Everyone looked at me to make the decision whether or not this was okay.

Mrs. Kennedy had no fear around animals of any kind, and she was an accomplished equestrian, so I said, "Sure. If Mrs. Kennedy wants to ride the camel, go ahead and let her ride the camel."

The photographers were going crazy, snapping pictures of the first lady and her sister high atop the camel, laughing like schoolgirls, as Bashir pulled the camel by a lead. Then I saw Mrs. Kennedy reach for the reins. Bashir and the handler went crazy.

"No, madame! No!" they yelled, the fear screaming from their eyes.

Sure enough, the camel became agitated and started thrashing as if he were going to take off in a gallop. The handler sprang into action to gain control, and poor Bashir looked like he was about to have a heart attack. Meanwhile, Mrs. Kennedy was laughing hysterically.

As Bashir regained control, I stepped in to assist Lee and Mrs. Kennedy as they dismounted the now very distressed camel.

It was a wonderful way to end the trip, and whenever I look at the pictures of Jacqueline Kennedy and her sister sitting sidesaddle on that camel, I still chuckle. Those images and memories are the epitome of who she was. Fun loving. Adventurous. Spontaneous. Down to earth and elegant at the same time.

Now, looking back sixty years, it seems almost impossible to believe Mrs. Kennedy was able to do the things she did back in 1962. She visited Lahore, Rawalpindi, Peshawar, and Karachi. Large, friendly crowds gathered along the roadways everywhere we traveled. Yet she never got credit for how

I rarely posed for photos, but I'm glad I did for this one in front of the officers' mess at the Khyber Rifles with Gordon Parks, from the White House Communications Agency.

103

Top: Mrs. Kennedy wasn't satisfied to have her photo taken next to the camel. She wanted to ride it. As Mrs. Kennedy and Lee climb aboard the seated camel, I stand back (with my arms folded), watching the animal's expression. He doesn't seem too happy, and I want to anticipate any sudden moves.

Bottom: Everything is going fine as Mrs. Kennedy and Lee sit calmly on top of the camel, posing with Bashir, the camel driver. This is the Associated Press photo that appeared in all the newspapers.

Top: But then Mrs. Kennedy grabs hold of the reins. The handler, at left, realizes this is not a good idea, and Bashir is holding on for dear life. He knows that if anything happens to Mrs. Kennedy, he will be disgraced in all of Pakistan.

Bottom: Sure enough, the camel becomes agitated. Lee begins shrieking, the attendant jumps in to assist, Bashir is about to have a heart attack— and Mrs. Kennedy is laughing hysterically.

Right: As Bashir regains control of the camel and commands it to kneel, I step in to assist the dismount. By this time, Lee is laughing along with Mrs. Kennedy, and the photographers are having a great time.

Opposite: Thousands came to the airport to bid farewell to Mrs. Kennedy the day she departed Pakistan. That's me in the center, smiling, as Mrs. Kennedy shares a final laugh with Ambassador McConaughy and Ayub Khan's military aide.

much she had helped the image of the United States in that part of the world and for the inspiration she gave to young girls and women.

In a UPI article that appeared in newspapers across America summarizing the trip, the reporter wrote:

"She had seen the Taj Mahal by moonlight, the burning and bathing ghats of the sacred Ganges River, pink Indian palaces and the grim Khyber Pass between Pakistan and Afghanistan. She had ridden an elephant and a camel and a bay gelding horse named Sardar, given her by President Ayub Khan."

And the final takeaway: "Three and four times a day she changed her costume, seldom appearing in the same dress twice."

At the time, I never thought much about the fact that we were taking the first lady through the Hindu-Kush mountains to the historic pass that connects Peshawar, in Pakistan, to Kabul, in Afghanistan. Now I realize what a truly unique and significant experience it was. In the ensuing years and decades, the security situation in that region gradually deteriorated to the point that entering the pass became inadvisable to anyone except military units. No American president or first lady has visited there since.

9

MRS. KENNEDY
& THE QUEEN

LONDON, 1962

On the way back from Pakistan in 1962, we flew via Pakistan International Airlines, first stopping in Tehran, Iran, where Mrs. Kennedy spent roughly forty-five minutes with the sister of the shah, and then flew on to London, where Mrs. Kennedy would stay for a few days at the home of Lee and Prince Radziwill, before returning to Washington. As was customary, the British ambassador to the United States, David Ormsby-Gore, had made certain the queen was aware that Mrs. Kennedy would be in London, and the queen promptly extended an invitation to Mrs. Kennedy for a private luncheon at Buckingham Palace.

The two women had met the previous year when President and Mrs. Kennedy stopped over in London, after Paris and Vienna, for the christening of the Radziwills' newborn baby daughter, Christina. During that visit, Queen Elizabeth II and Prince Philip held a formal dinner in their honor at Buckingham Palace.

Opposite: President Kennedy, Queen Elizabeth II, Mrs. Kennedy, and Prince Philip at Buckingham Palace, 1961.

Left: Mrs. Kennedy and Queen Elizabeth II when they first met at Buckingham Palace, in 1961.

As we drove from the airport into central London, Mrs. Kennedy suddenly said, "Mr. Hill, did you know that I was at Queen Elizabeth's coronation?"

Sitting in the front left passenger seat of the British limousine, I turned around to face her. "No, Mrs. Kennedy, I did not know that. So, this will be your third meeting with her?"

She laughed. "No, I didn't actually meet her at the coronation. I was working as a photographer for the *Washington Times-Herald* and I convinced them to send me over to London to cover it. Much as I tried, I didn't get anywhere near her. Who would have thought I'd be invited to lunch with her, all on my own, all these years later?"

"It certainly says something about how much respect she has for you, Mrs. Kennedy," I said.

In fact, the queen and Mrs. Kennedy seemed to me to have quite a lot in common and were just three years apart in age. Queen Elizabeth was thirty-five at the time, and Mrs. Kennedy was thirty-two. They'd both been thrust onto the world stage at a relatively young age, both had young children, both loved horses and dogs, and both coveted the privacy of their family life. I imagined their conversation would flow easily.

The Radziwill residence was a four-story brick town house located at 4 Buckingham Place, a short distance from the gates of Buckingham Palace. The front door opened directly onto the sidewalk, adjacent to the street, and even though the British police had officers guarding the door, the British press and an ever-changing landscape of gawkers had set up camp all around the area.

Shortly before we were to leave for the luncheon, I warned Mrs. Kennedy about the situation outside.

"The car is parked directly in front of the residence," I said, "but there is quite a crowd, the neighbors are hanging out the windows on all sides, and as soon as you walk out the door, the press are going to go crazy."

"All right, Mr. Hill," she said. "I'll be prepared."

A crowd had gathered outside the Radziwill residence, waiting for Mrs. Kennedy to emerge prior to her luncheon with the queen. She graciously smiles for the cameras before getting into the car. Notice the neighbors hanging out of the windows overhead.

Sure enough, as soon as the door opened, it was a barrage of flashes and the *click-click-click* of several dozen camera shutters going off at once.

"How do you feel about having lunch with the queen, Mrs. Kennedy?" someone shouted.

Mrs. Kennedy smiled, and as I guided her toward the car, she said, "It's a great honor to be going to the palace."

Just as I opened the back door for her to get in, a photographer shouted, "Wave, Mrs. Kennedy!"

Without missing a beat, she looked at the man and said sweetly, "Why should I wave? I'm not leaving yet."

And with that, she ducked into the back seat. I closed the door and took my place in the left front seat, and off we went to Buckingham Palace. She didn't say anything during the short ride, but I could tell she was both excited about this unique opportunity, and a bit nervous about such an important visit without her husband by her side. We drove to the palace gates and into the palace, where there were attendants to meet the car. Once inside the palace gates, I knew Mrs. Kennedy was under the protection of the British government, and since I was not invited to have lunch with the queen, I waited outside with the car and driver as Mrs. Kennedy was escorted inside.

The two spent less than two hours together, and when Mrs. Kennedy got back into the car, her anxiety had disappeared and she seemed completely relaxed.

"So how was your lunch with the queen, Mrs. Kennedy?" I asked as we made the short drive back to the Radziwills'.

"Oh, it was delightful," she said. "We talked about India and our children, and after a while, we were just two mothers."

Private luncheons between heads of state and guests are meant to be private, and Mrs. Kennedy was well aware that anything she might say publicly could be wildly misconstrued by the press. As expected, hundreds of people were still gathered outside the residence, and as soon as she stepped out of the car, before I could intervene, a television reporter had thrust a microphone toward her.

When Mrs. Kennedy returned from her private luncheon with Queen Elizabeth, she was close-lipped about what was discussed, until she went inside. Stash Radziwill at left, Lee Radziwill inside the doorway, Mrs. Kennedy, and me, staring down one of the encroaching reporters.

"Mrs. Kennedy, for British television, did you enjoy a really good lunch? An English lunch?"

"Yes." She smiled as she turned and walked toward the front door. "I did. Thank you very much."

The reporter persisted. "Tell me, how did the queen seem?"

"Her Majesty was so kind to have me there," Mrs. Kennedy answered. "I don't think I should say anything about it except how grateful I am and how charming she was."

I could tell she didn't want to engage with the reporters, so I gently touched her elbow and said, "Let's go inside, Mrs. Kennedy."

Lee was waiting in the foyer and could hardly wait to grab hold of her sister. "Tell me everything!" she said. I kept my distance as Mrs. Kennedy regaled her sister with every detail of her lunch with the queen: what Her Majesty was wearing; what they ate and drank; the table setting with its china, flowers, and glassware; and, of course, every morsel of their conversation. Mrs. Kennedy knew her sister wouldn't betray her trust.

Other than lunch with the queen, the stopover in London was merely to be a few days of relaxation before returning to the United States. One particularly memorable evening, Mrs. Kennedy and Lee gathered some friends together at the Radziwill residence. Benno Graziani was there, as well as Oleg Cassini, the designer who created so many of her outfits for that trip. The champagne was flowing and everyone was really letting loose. Mrs. Kennedy and Lee were regaling everyone with details from the trip, and at one point Mrs. Kennedy brought out the long garlands she'd been given in India and ceremoniously draped them around Cassini's and Graziani's necks.

I stayed out of the way, peeking in every now and then just to make sure I knew what was going on. It was wonderful to see her so relaxed, sharing an evening laughing and dancing with close friends. For those few hours, surrounded by people she'd known long before she became an international icon, she could just be Jackie.

It was on that trip that she said something to me I'll never forget. It was just her and Lee and Stash lounging in the living room. "Come join us, Mr. Hill," she invited. "We're telling Stash what a wonderful trip he missed."

Top: At the party at the Radziwill residence in London, on the way home from our trip to India and Pakistan, Mrs. Kennedy poses with Benno Graziani (left) and Oleg Cassini (right), who are goofing around with the necklaces and garlands given to her and Lee in India.

Bottom: Lee and Mrs. Kennedy playing charades at the Radziwill home in London. Mrs. Kennedy was able to let loose when she was with her friends in private. This was a wild, fun night.

They were all smoking, and I suppose I probably lit up a cigarette myself. We talked about the Khyber Pass and their impromptu camel ride.

"Poor Bashir," I said. "You should have seen the look on his face when you reached for the reins. I doubt he'd ever seen two women in short dresses with high heels sitting sidesaddle on his camel before."

They all laughed. "And," I continued, "he was scared to death you were going to tumble off and he'd be held responsible. Banished and never to be heard from again."

We sat there, smoking and laughing, and as Mrs. Kennedy was recalling some palace or some facet of Islamic architecture she found incredibly fascinating, I must not have responded the way she expected. She turned to me and said, "Doesn't anything ever impress you, Mr. Hill?"

I can still see her: The cigarette dangling casually between her fingers. The twinkle in her eyes. That unmistakable whispery voice.

I looked right into her eyes and said with a smile, "I guess it takes a lot to impress me, Mrs. Kennedy."

Throughout the entire journey, Mrs. Kennedy didn't grant any interviews to the press, other than the brief comments she'd give when they were following her from one public site to the next. On the flight from London back to Washington, her friend Joan Braden, a journalist who had been on the entire trip, practically begged Mrs. Kennedy to let her sit with her on this last leg so she could get some information for the article she'd promised her magazine. I was sitting behind them and could hear the entire conversation.

At one point, Joan commented that she was impressed with how much history Mrs. Kennedy knew.

"I'd never heard of Emperor Akbar until I started reading for the trip," Mrs. Kennedy admitted. "But that's why I think travel is so important and I'll always care so much about student exchanges. Not only does it teach you about the past, but once you've been among the people and gotten to know some of them, their problems are so much more real to you than they are from home, and you become more sympathetic."

Every so often, she'd comment on how "the Secret Service wouldn't allow me to do" this or that while she was in India. They were things Agent Jeffries had forbidden after I'd left, and of course she knew I was sitting right behind her.

"When we were riding around the lake in Udaipur, I wanted to stop at the ghats and get out and say hello to the people who were standing and waving all along the shore. But by the time the boat stopped, hundreds of people were there and the Secret Service wouldn't let me get out."

I'd catch her glancing surreptitiously between the seats to see if I was listening, but I'd be looking down or out the window, pretending not to be paying attention. It was her way of telling me what had gone wrong without bad-mouthing Agent Jeffries directly.

She talked about Prime Minister Nehru and how impressed she was with him. "He was terribly good to us," she said. "He spent an hour or so each day walking in the gardens with Lee and me."

"What did you talk about?" Joan asked.

"Nothing serious, really," she said. "I guess because Jack has always told me the one thing a busy man doesn't want to talk about at the end of the day is whether the Geneva Conference will be successful or what settlement could be made in Kashmir or anything like that."

On Ambassador Galbraith, she said, "Ken really was a saint on the whole trip. He is really rather witty. Whenever we were so tired and thought we couldn't take another step, he always made us laugh and gave us the courage to go on."

When the discussion moved on to Pakistan, Mrs. Kennedy was even more exuberant.

"Oh, Pakistan was wonderful, didn't you think? And Ayub Khan—he's just like Jack," she said. "Tough and brave and wants things done in a hurry."

She talked about how he'd given her his hat to wear. "And then Lee and I bought gray and brown ones too."

She turned around and said, "Mr. Hill, do you know where the hats are?"

I had no idea where the hats were. I did a lot of extra things for her, but packing was not one of them. Before I could answer, she said, "Maybe I can talk Jack into wearing one off the plane when he meets me!"

We all laughed at the thought of President Kennedy in Ayub Khan's karakul cap.

"I'm willing to bet that's one thing you won't be able to get the president to do, Mrs. Kennedy," I said.

"I know," she laughed. "But the thought of it!"

Toward the end of the flight, when we could feel the plane slowly losing altitude, Mrs. Kennedy raised her voice level a bit. "Although I sometimes fret about the Secret Service," she said, "I don't know what we'd do without them."

It was obvious she wanted me to hear this part of the conversation. "They are usually right, and every single one of them is so kind and dedicated and bright. Every president and his family must drive them mad, as it's such an adjustment to go from private life to constant surveillance."

"Of course, they are there for your well-being and security," Joan said.

"Oh, yes," Mrs. Kennedy acknowledged. She added, "When the Secret Service tries to stop Jack from doing things, he just says No and shakes hands with whomever he wants and does what he wants." She glanced to see if I was paying attention, then added with a smile, "But usually I can't get away with it."

From that point on, everything was different with Mrs. Kennedy and me. I knew she'd been the one to have Jeffries removed and me promoted to be the Special Agent in Charge of her detail. We had developed a good rapport, a bond based on trust and mutual respect. As time went on, that bond just grew stronger and stronger.

Shortly before we'd left London, Mrs. Kennedy asked me if I'd bought any souvenirs or gifts on the trip.

"No, Mrs. Kennedy," I said. "I didn't have much time to go shopping."

"Oh, that's such a shame," she said. "You should have something to give to your wife when you get home."

Before I could say anything, she said, "Wait here."

She returned with a dark mauve-purple silk scarf. "I've got more silk than I know what to do with," she said as she handed it to me. "Wrap this up nicely and I'm sure she'll appreciate that you thought of her while you were away."

At some point during the last few days of the trip, I got an urgent message from General Godfrey McHugh asking me to call him on a secure line.

"Clint," he said, "do you know anything about a horse that was given to Mrs. Kennedy by Ayub Khan?"

"Yes, I sure do," I said.

"Well, the president has tasked me with getting the damn thing back to Washington. It has to avoid quarantine and he was adamant there be no publicity about this. I mean, he was so insistent, if anything comes out about this, there will be hell to pay."

I was glad McHugh couldn't see the smile on my face as he was explaining his problem. Godfrey McHugh was one of three high-ranking military officers—along with Navy captain Taz Shepard and Army general Ted Clifton—assigned to the White House military aide's office, and I worked with him frequently. McHugh was a nice enough guy, and because of his rank and appointed position in the White House, he could make things happen, but he was desperately afraid of making a mistake. There was a meekness about him, such that in situations like this I'd seen him quaking like a timorous schoolboy.

"Understood. What can I do to help?" I offered.

"I've got an Air Force C-41 in Lahore that's going to bring the horse back. But we can't have any paperwork that says there's a horse on the plane. It's coming back to the States for routine maintenance. We need as few people as possible involved, and President Kennedy told me I should keep you informed and advised if there were any problems."

"Yes, General, please do."

Once the horse was on the plane, there was one thing after another. The route had to be changed midair because when they affirmed there was a horse on the plane, the country in which they were planning to land for refueling wouldn't let them open the doors for fear that a horse from Pakistan could be bringing in disease-carrying flies. I thought McHugh was going to have a nervous breakdown over this horse.

There had already been so much publicity about Sardar that McHugh couldn't avoid the U.S. Agriculture Department. But as soon as Ag got involved, they were insisting the horse had to go into quarantine in Philadelphia in some special kind of stable. McHugh finally convinced some high-ranking official at Agriculture that this was such a top-secret operation that the plane was going to land at Andrews Air Force Base no matter what and Agriculture would just have to send an official—who would be sworn to secrecy—to check out the horse. Once the horse arrived, though, he'd have to stay at a special stable at Fort Myer for at least fifteen days before he could be transported to the Kennedys' rented house, Glen Ora, in Middleburg, Virginia.

When the plane finally landed at Andrews in the middle of the night, McHugh went out to meet the Agriculture inspector and to make sure the press didn't get wind of anything. It happened to be Easter weekend and I was with the Kennedys in Palm Beach, asleep in my motel room, when the phone rang.

"Clint! It's Godfrey. I'm here at Andrews with Mrs. Kennedy's horse."

"Wonderful," I said. "Is he in good shape?"

"The horse is fine. But he's not alone."

"What do you mean?"

"There's a man here that's dressed like a maharajah of Jaipur—he's wearing a red coat with medals and ribbons all over it and a damn turban on his head! When I asked him who the hell he was, he says, 'I come with Sardar. President Ayub Khan's orders. I cannot leave Sardar.'

"And then," McHugh continued, in a voice that sounded like his veins were popping out of his neck, "the inspector sees a bunch of hay in the compartment, and when the horse's guard tells him that's the only thing the horse will eat, the inspector goes berserk.

"He tells us we've got to burn the hay, confiscate the horse's water, and spray down the whole goddamn plane!"

I was trying not to laugh, but the image in my head of McHugh, an Air Force general, out there in the middle of the night on this covert equine mission, following direct orders from the president of the United States, all because Mrs. Kennedy couldn't stand the thought of her beautiful horse in quarantine, was hysterical.

"Calm down, General," I said. "Just tell me this: Where is the horse now?"

"The horse and his guard are about to be transported to Fort Myer. The horse has to stay in a special stable for fifteen days before he can be let out. How the hell are we going to keep this quiet when there's a guy with a turban walking around Fort Myer?"

"Look," I said, "we'll deal with any fallout if it leaks. Just make sure nothing happens to that horse."

As soon as we got back to Washington, Mrs. Kennedy couldn't wait to go see Sardar.

I took her and Caroline out to Fort Myer, in Arlington, and lo and behold, the Pakistani guard walked out, in full military regalia, leading Sardar by the reins. Mrs. Kennedy wasn't dressed to ride—General McHugh had told her she absolutely could not ride the horse for at least two more weeks, preferably thirty days—but she was delighted to see that Sardar was healthy and to show Caroline the new addition to their animal menagerie.

Mrs. Kennedy and Caroline visit Sardar at Fort Myer while the horse is quarantined. We were under strict orders from President Kennedy not to allow any photos of the surreptitious visit to be released.

It was comical to see the Pakistani guard in full military regalia barring Mrs. Kennedy from even touching her beloved horse for fear of violating the quarantine rules of the U.S. Agriculture Department. She grabs hold of the reins and promises Sardar he'll be out of quarantine soon.

White House photographer Cecil Stoughton came along to record the momentous event—with strict instructions from President Kennedy that the photos were not to be released. It was wonderful to see Mrs. Kennedy so happy, but mostly I was relieved to see that the horse had come through his ordeal none the worse for wear.

A few days later, Mrs. Kennedy showed up in my office at the White House in her riding gear and said, "Mr. Hill, I'd like to go to Fort Myer." It wasn't my job to tell her what she could or could not do. I didn't work for the Agriculture Department.

When Sardar was finally released and transported to Middleburg, I received a type-written memo from Cecil Stoughton:

MEMORANDUM FOR MRS. J.F. KENNEDY
THRU MR. CLINT HILL
FOLLOWING IS THE LIST OF NAMES OF THE MEN INSTRUMENTAL
IN THE CARE AND FEEDING OF SARDAR.

He'd listed ten men—three colonels, two lieutenant colonels, a captain, two lieutenants, and two privates first class—who had secretly taken care of Sardar at Fort Myer.

At the bottom he had added a handwritten note:

the pictures will be ready Friday 11 May.

Mrs. Kennedy had obviously asked Stoughton to make some enlargements, which she would autograph and include with thank-you notes to the individuals for all they'd done under the deep cloak of secrecy. I gave her the memorandum and thought nothing more of it.

The next day I found Stoughton's memo on my desk. At the top, she'd handwritten:

Mr. Hill—Could you <u>please</u> learn to do my signature

It was a request she'd made to me many times, only half in jest. She would spend hours signing photographs of herself or of her and the president, which he had also signed, and I always carried a stack of them with me to hand out to flight attendants or staff who had been especially helpful on trips.

I did a lot of things for Mrs. Kennedy, but I knew that if I gave in to her once, it would be an ongoing thing. This was one task I was not going to take on. She may have been able to convince someone else to sign her photographs, but it wasn't me.

10

LATIN AMERICA

1961–1962

Finding all the memorabilia I had saved from my travels with Mrs. Kennedy had not only sparked a lot of memories, but as I thought about all the places we went and the impact she made, it was rather remarkable. There was no formal job requirement for the spouse of the president of the United States, and each one—to this point it had always been a woman—had created her own version of the role. Mrs. Kennedy had no interest in politics, but in just three years in the White House, she proved herself to be, arguably, one of the best ambassadors the United States has ever had. After that first triumphant visit to Paris, enchanting de Gaulle, she made similar splashes in Greece, England, Italy, at the Vatican, and in the dueling countries of India and Pakistan. Her fluency in multiple languages combined with her understanding of world history and unmatched charisma proved to be one of the president's secret weapons on the international front. She embraced that role, not to further any personal agenda, but entirely to support her husband. I don't think she ever truly understood how, or why, people admired her so. But I saw it, and perhaps more than anywhere else, she was beloved in Latin America.

One of President Kennedy's landmark policies was the Alliance for Progress—a program to improve relations and foster economic development, social progress, and political freedom in Latin America. In December of '61 we went on a whirlwind goodwill trip to Puerto Rico, Venezuela, and Colombia—all Spanish-speaking and predominantly Catholic. The people loved this first-ever Catholic U.S. president and the fact that his wife spoke Spanish—my God, that was political gold.

From the moment we arrived in San Juan, everywhere we went there were huge crowds chanting *"Viva President Kennedy! Viva President Kennedy!"* Infrequently, there were pockets of anti-American protesters where KENNEDY, No! was scrawled on a few billboards, but right next to the graffiti was painted JACKIE, SÍ!

After the traditional motorcade in Caracas, we helicoptered to a rural region where the aid money was going to build homes for farmers. President and Mrs. Kennedy both enjoyed going into situations like this where they could shake hands and spend a few moments with ordinary citizens. At a ribbon-cutting ceremony, President Kennedy's remarks were translated, and then he invited Mrs. Kennedy to say a few words. As she spoke to the group in Spanish, having memorized a short speech—with no notes—President Kennedy stood by her side, beaming with pride.

In Bogotá, at a dinner for four hundred guests in the San Carlos Palace, President Kennedy confessed that he didn't speak Spanish but that he had brought along a translator. He turned to Mrs. Kennedy and said, "My wife, Jacqueline."

The room erupted as she stepped up to the microphone and spoke, in effortless Spanish, about how education, housing, and employment should be within reach of all and not just a few blessed by fortune.

Six months after that trip, at the end of June 1962, President and Mrs. Kennedy made a high-profile state visit to Mexico that further symbolized the president's sincere focus on improving relations with our neighbors to the south. Two million people lined the motorcade route from the airport into Mexico City, cheering and waving Mexican and American flags. As we slowly weaved through the heart of the city, red, white, and blue confetti poured down from the high-rise buildings like a blizzard until it filled the open cars up to the windows. It was incredible.

President Kennedy looks on with pride as Mrs. Kennedy speaks in Spanish at a ribbon-cutting ceremony near Caracas, Venezuela. Speaking without notes, she connected with the ordinary citizens in a way that the remarks by the president, through a translator, could not.

In our motorcade through Mexico City—that's JFK standing
in an open car with President Adolfo López Mateos—we
traveled through a blizzard of confetti. Two million people
lined the route, and by the time we got to the end, the
cars were filled to the rim with red, white, and blue shards
of paper. The outpouring of affection for this first-ever
Catholic president and his Spanish-speaking wife was
unlike anything I'd ever seen.

There were the usual official meetings, dinners, and cultural tours, and everywhere we went, Mrs. Kennedy spoke in Spanish. There was always a State Department interpreter around, and while many of the Mexican dignitaries also spoke English, you could see their eyes light up when Mrs. Kennedy leaned in and spoke to them in their native tongue. At one function, she stepped up to the microphone and said, in Spanish: "Mexico has left a permanent impact in the mind and the culture of the world today. The ancient spirit of Mexico is what has not changed; this makes us remember that economic progress can be achieved without destroying the values of the heart and the human mind."

President Adolfo López Mateos and President Kennedy look on admiringly as Mrs. Kennedy delivers a speech in flawless Spanish at a luncheon in Mexico City. Her ability to connect to the people in their native language broke down barriers and endeared her to the people of Mexico.

She had put a lot of effort into practicing her accent and pronunciation to ensure her words were understood, and you could tell by the expressions on the faces of those in the audience that she was connecting. Breaking into a big smile, she ended with a rousing *"Viva México!"*

Everyone in the room jumped to their feet with enthusiastic applause. In those few short moments, she had captured their hearts.

The morning of Sunday, July 1, President and Mrs. Kennedy attended Mass at the Basílica de Guadalupe, led by the archbishop primate of Mexico City. As the first Catholic president and first lady, their attendance at the Mass in Mexico symbolized the depth of their feelings for the Mexican people and the friendship between our two countries.

Later that year, we were in Palm Beach for Christmas. On December 29, we flew to Miami on the presidential helicopter to the Orange Bowl so that President and Mrs. Kennedy could publicly honor 1,113 Bay of Pigs survivors who had just been freed by Fidel Castro. It was the result of months of negotiations, and once again, President Kennedy had asked Mrs. Kennedy to say a few words in Spanish.

Some forty thousand people had filled the Orange Bowl to welcome home the brave freedom fighters, many of whom were missing limbs. It was an emotional ceremony, during which President Kennedy was presented the brigade's war-torn flag that had flown during the three-day battle at the Bay of Pigs. It was rare for President and Mrs. Kennedy to appear together in public like this, so when Mrs. Kennedy stepped before the microphones and gave a short speech in Spanish, with no notes, the crowd went wild.

Mrs. Kennedy's ability to speak the language in so many countries we visited endeared both her and the president and, by extension, all Americans to the people of those nations. And for the immigrants and refugees who had left their homelands desperate for a better life in the United States, when Mrs. Kennedy spoke in their native language, it was a validation of their worth.

More than forty thousand people jammed the Orange Bowl to see President and Mrs. Kennedy when they welcomed back the Bay of Pigs survivors in December 1962. The crowd erupted in cheers as we departed, following Mrs. Kennedy's heartfelt speech in Spanish to the largely Spanish-speaking Cuban American audience. That's me in sunglasses at the rear of the car. Despite the friendliness of the crowd, those situations were particularly nerve-racking in pre-magnetometer times.

11

—

MIDDLEBURG

—

ALEXANDRIA, VIRGINIA, 2019

Each day, Lisa and I would return to the house at 1068 North Chambliss, tackling one portion of the basement at a time. It was exhausting, mentally and physically, to go through everything.

There was a closet under the stairs in the basement that I had yet to look into. *God knows what's in here*, I thought. I turned the handle and pulled, but the door was stuck. Clearly, it hadn't been opened in a long time. After a few hard tugs, it finally opened. There was no light, but I could see two large open boxes that were shoved against the back wall. I bent over and dragged one of the boxes out of the closet to get a better look.

Well, what do you know?

The box was filled with framed photos of all shapes and sizes. As I pulled the top picture out of the box and saw the one lying beneath it, I couldn't help but smile. Two photos of Mrs. Kennedy riding in Middleburg. The horse wasn't Sardar—this was before she'd been to Pakistan—it was Bit of Irish. The photos had been professionally framed, with identical moss-green mats and gold frames, both signed and inscribed in white ink by the photographer, Marshall Hawkins. Never hung on the wall, they'd been protected from light by the darkness of the closet. Covered in dust but otherwise in perfect condition.

The larger of the two photos showed Mrs. Kennedy sitting rod-straight atop a beautiful chestnut-brown horse, in hunting riding attire: a black blazer with form-fitting beige riding pants tucked into black leather boots and a bowler snug on top of her head. The horse is in motion, appearing as if it were walking slowly. Mrs. Kennedy has a contented smile on her face, her white-gloved hands holding the reins tight, confidently, and in complete control of the beautiful horse beneath her. The inscription reads:

Mrs. John F. Kennedy
Hunting with Orange County, The Plains, Virginia
March 1961

The other photo, slightly smaller, was far more interesting. Mrs. Kennedy is in similar riding clothes, but in this moment captured in time the horse has stopped dead in its tracks behind a timber post-and-rail fence. Mrs. Kennedy is the one in motion, diving headfirst over the front of the horse, her body taut in a straight line from head to toes, upside down in midair, legs straight toward the sky, her white-gloved hands outstretched toward the ground, which is still a good three-feet below, bracing for the inevitable hard landing.

The inscription on this one reads:

Mrs. John F. Kennedy comes a cropper
while hunting with Piedmont
November, 1961

The framed photos had been delivered to me at the White House, and I remember having to look up what "comes a cropper" meant. I might not have understood the proper terminology, but I sure as hell knew what I wanted to do with that photographer. He had jumped suddenly out from the trees to snap a photograph, and that had caused the horse to stop dead in its tracks, sending Mrs. Kennedy flying headfirst over the fence. If she wasn't such a good athlete, she could have been badly injured, paralyzed, or even killed. Much to my relief, Mrs. Kennedy got right back up on the horse and I had a few choice words for Marshall Hawkins.

Photographer Marshall Hawkins gave me this autographed and framed photo. He caused the horrifying incident by scaring the horse and ended up making money from the photograph.

Mrs. John F. Kennedy comes a cropper
while hunting with Piedmont
November, 1961

Photo by Marshall Hawkins
Warrenton, Virginia

After working in the house all day, by six o'clock Lisa and I were both tired, dirty, and hungry. We'd found a few things of interest but had also filled at least ten giant garbage bags of stuff that would either be tossed or donated.

Back at the Willard, we got cleaned up and headed down to the Round Robin Bar for a drink and casual dinner. After the server took our orders, I said, "I came across something I almost tossed out. It's really nothing important, but I thought I'd better show it to you first."

I reached into my pocket and pulled out my wallet.

I knew her impatience was building with every second, so I deliberately held the wallet on the table for a moment before flipping through the clear plastic pages, pretending I didn't know exactly where I'd stuck the discovery.

"I found these in a manila envelope tucked in the back of one of my desk drawers," I said as I pulled out the three unlaminated cards.

I handed one of them to her, knowing this was exactly the kind of thing she loved: pieces of history she could actually touch.

"Oh my God," she whispered. " 'Virginia State Non-Resident License to Hunt Only. Fifteen dollars and seventy-five cents. July 1, 1962, to June 30, 1963. Mrs. Jacqueline Kennedy, Washington, D.C. Color: W.' "

She looked up at me. " 'W' for 'white'? Did they really put down the color of your skin on your hunting license?"

"It was a different time," I said.

She continued reading the rest of the card. " 'Age thirty-three. Height five foot seven. County of Fauquier. Date issued September 28, 1962. Signed Jacqueline B. Kennedy.'

"So cool!" Lisa exclaimed. It never ceases to amaze me how excited she gets over the most mundane things.

"Did Jackie Kennedy really need to present a form of identification to hunt?" she asked.

"Oh, they didn't care who you were or what your pedigree was," I said with a laugh. "Those hunts were—and I suppose still are—serious business."

"So why did you have it?"

"Well, you know how you are always setting your phone down somewhere and you can't remember where you left it?"

"And then you pick it up and put it in your pocket so you'll have it when I need it," Lisa said with a smile.

"Exactly," I said.

Middleburg was Mrs. Kennedy's happy place. When she first told me that she and the president had rented a home about fifty miles from the White House as a weekend retreat, I couldn't imagine why. The president and his family had access to Camp David, which had all the accoutrements and activities one would want, with complete privacy, so it made no sense to me that they'd need another place so close to Washington. The reason, I quickly realized, was Mrs. Kennedy's passion for horseback riding and fox hunting.

Glen Ora, the estate the Kennedys had rented, contained a stately six-bedroom home that dated back to the nineteenth century, a large swimming pool, tennis court, and, most important of all, horse stables and four hundred sweeping acres on which she could gallop to her heart's content, with no access for prying photographers. It was surrounded by other similar estates owned by wealthy families like the Mellons and the du Ponts, all separated by winding country roads and miles of wood fences that marked property lines and provided countless jumping opportunities for the riders of the hunts.

Also nearby was a close friend of Mrs. Kennedy's named Eve Fout. Eve and her husband, Paul, shared Mrs. Kennedy's endless enthusiasm for horses and were members of the exclusive Orange County Hunt Club. The club was so select that it had once turned down the duke of Windsor to ride as a guest. The sole reason Mrs. Kennedy was invited to join had nothing to do with her position as first lady; it was because she was such a skilled horsewoman. Her favorite horse belonged to the Fouts, a brown and white paint called Rufus, which she tried repeatedly to buy from them. Lots of people wouldn't have said no to Jackie Kennedy, but the Fouts refused to sell Rufus. Mrs. Kennedy settled on purchasing another horse named Bit of Irish and promptly began participating in the club's activities. You could tell she was comfortable in this environment—she knew the proper attire to wear for the various hunts, she spoke the cryptic language effortlessly discussing hounds and hill topping and whippers-in—and she thrived on the camaraderie.

Mrs. Kennedy had few female friends, but Eve Fout was definitely one of her closest confidantes. The two had been acquaintances since they were teenagers, having met through horse shows and competitions. They were almost exactly the same age and they spoke with the same soft voice that seemed to have been cultivated at the private girls' schools they'd attended. While they were both socially shy, I could see a noticeable difference in Mrs. Kennedy's demeanor when she was with Eve. There was no pretense, no need for small talk or polite chatter when they were together, almost like she could slip back into that time when she was Jacqueline Bouvier. Everything revolved around the children, horses, hounds, and

Mrs. Kennedy felt completely relaxed around her hunt club friends in Middleburg. She was just like one of them—except that she always had a couple of Secret Service agents lurking around. I am apparently not too pleased with some activity going on behind Mrs. Kennedy as she chats with one of her friends.

fox hunting. While Mrs. Kennedy was a woman of few words, with Eve and Paul, her dry sense of humor came out frequently with wry one-liners that would send everyone into hysterical laughter.

It became routine for us to spend almost every weekend in Middleburg during the hunting season, from mid-autumn to late spring. At first, we'd go on a Friday, the president would fly in by helicopter on Saturday, and everyone would leave together Sunday afternoon. But it wasn't long before Mrs. Kennedy became entrenched in the hunt activities, and the weekends for her would often stretch from Thursday to the following Tuesday. When the president left town, so did the press. So Mrs. Kennedy could walk with Caroline in downtown Middleburg—a single street lined with antique shops, two-hundred-year-old taverns, and an eclectic toy and gift store called the Fun Shop—and almost feel like a normal person. I'd be close by, always just a few steps behind her, but it was remarkable that, unlike everywhere else we went, the people in Middleburg treated her like she was just another resident. They were polite and would say, "Good afternoon," in passing; there was no gawking, no screaming mobs clamoring to touch her.

I soon realized that part of the reason Mrs. Kennedy wanted to spend time in the Virginia Hunt Country was so that she could teach Caroline to ride proficiently, with the hope she would love all things equestrian as much as her mother. But more than anything else it was a place where she could try to give her children as normal an upbringing as possible, despite the fact that they would always be the children of a president.

President and Mrs. Kennedy bought a pony named Macaroni from the Brittle family and he became Caroline's. (It always irks me when I read somewhere that Macaroni was a gift from Lyndon B. Johnson. It's incorrect: LBJ did give Caroline a pony a couple of years later, but that one was named Tex.) Caroline was just three years old that spring of 1961 when we first went to Middleburg, and I must say, seeing how relaxed Mrs. Kennedy was with her young daughter sitting in the saddle on top of a pony that had a mind of its own caused me a great deal of concern. It wasn't my job to parent, but I knew I would feel somewhat responsible if the child fell and got seriously injured. Mrs. Kennedy, though, had such an ease about the way she sat Caroline on the horse and calmly gave her instructions.

Mrs. Kennedy enrolled Caroline in the Middleburg Orange County Pony Club so she could take riding lessons and meet some of the other young children in the area. There was a class called the lead-line class, in which the mothers walked alongside their children on their ponies, leading them around a short course. It was all very informal, with the club meetings held at various members' properties. BYOP: Bring Your Own Pony.

Mrs. Kennedy would show up wearing trousers and boots and, depending on the weather, often covered in an oversized raincoat. Here no one was focused on her clothing; she was just another mother sharing her love of horses and riding with her young daughter.

The older children in the club were often assigned to the younger ones to help teach the rules of the hunt when they went "beagling"—the children's version of fox hunting in which the parents hold loosely to a line attached to the pony, with their youngster straddled atop learning to guide with the reins. A pack of floppy-eared beagles replace the excitable scent-driven hounds, chasing an oblivious bunny rabbit instead of an elusive fox.

One of Caroline's mentors was Page Allen, a girl six years older. Page and her older sister, Betsy, were avid and accomplished riders, and their father, Howard Allen, who was a local photographer, was always around with a couple of cameras strapped around his neck taking photos. One day he took a few candid shots of Mrs. Kennedy and Caroline and brought the prints to Mrs. Kennedy the next day.

"Mrs. Kennedy," Howard said, "I took some photos of you and Caroline and I thought you'd like to have them."

Mrs. Kennedy shared her love of horses and riding with Caroline from an early age. Here she is in 1961, when Caroline was just three, riding one of her favorite horses, a beautiful paint named Rufus.

Top: Caroline was just three years old when Mrs. Kennedy enrolled her in the Middleburg Orange County Pony Club. You can see the joy on Mrs. Kennedy's face as she walks alongside Caroline on her pony Macaroni in the lead-line at the 1961 Apple Barrel Show.

Bottom: Three-year-old Caroline is intent on her pony's footwork as Mrs. Kennedy leads a skittish Macaroni over the beginner's jump. It wasn't my job to parent, but it did concern me that Mrs. Kennedy was so relaxed with her young daughter atop this animal with a mind of its own.

This photo by Howard Allen was one of Mrs. Kennedy's favorites. More than anything, she wanted her children to have a "normal" life, and in this photo, if she wasn't the most recognized woman in the world, you might see just a mother with her two children, walking through the mucky grass in their riding boots.

He handed her the photos and she broke into a huge smile. "Oh, Mr. Allen, they're wonderful!" she said.

"I know you've requested the media not to publish photos of the children," he quickly interjected. "So of course I won't. You have my word on that."

Both Caroline and Mrs. Kennedy adored Page Allen. On frequent occasions, Mrs. Kennedy would invite Page to Glen Ora, offering to send a driver with a trailer to pick up Page's pony so the two girls could ride together. She was so concerned about giving Caroline a "normal" life out of the spotlight, and Middleburg, in so many ways, provided that.

When President and Mrs. Kennedy first began spending
weekends in Middleburg, there was no official Catholic
church, so Sunday Mass was held at the Middleburg
Community Center. Whenever the president and
Mrs. Kennedy were in town, there would be a large crowd
of local residents waiting outside to greet them. Here
Mrs. Kennedy smiles with recognition at Howard Allen as
he snaps this photo, which also includes his daughters,
Page (far left) and Betsy (with camera), who were riding
friends of Caroline's.

Mrs. Kennedy invited the pony club to Glen Ora one Sunday for a beagling so she could show her husband and her sister Lee, who was visiting from London, how Caroline was learning to ride with the hunt. It was the first time a president of the United States had come to watch, and it was undoubtedly the highest-attended meet of the season.

At one point, Mrs. Kennedy invited the pony club for a Sunday beagling at Glen Ora. I'm pretty sure it was the highest attendance of any of their meets, with many more parents showing up to watch and participate than I'd seen previously. Of course, they were hoping President Kennedy might be there, and indeed he was, along with Mrs. Kennedy's sister Lee, who was visiting from London.

Wearing his brown leather Air Force One flight jacket, President Kennedy stood behind a fence watching with delight as the parents and children gathered on their horses and ponies.

Mrs. Kennedy was so pleased to be able to show her husband and sister the progress Caroline had made and how she interacted with the other riders. No photographers were allowed except Howard Allen.

The Allen family really became part of Mrs. Kennedy's inner circle in Middleburg. They were an average family—Howard's wife, Nancy, owned the Fun

Shop, which Mrs. Kennedy frequented, and their two daughters were wonderful playmates for Caroline.

One Monday in November 1962, Mrs. Kennedy informed me that she had invited Howard Allen to Glen Ora to take some photos of her riding with Caroline and John. She came out of the house dressed in a creamy white turtleneck cable-knit sweater and slim trousers tucked into Western boots. Caroline had on a colorful red jacket, which contrasted with her black riding helmet, and John was bundled up in a light blue jacket with matching pants. Mrs. Kennedy had an artistic eye, and undoubtedly, the complementing outfits had been carefully chosen.

Howard had come equipped with two cameras, one filled with black-and-white film, the other with color. He walked around getting various angles as Mrs. Kennedy rode with John in front of her atop Sardar, the horse given to her by President Ayub Khan of Pakistan, and Caroline on Macaroni.

When President Ayub Khan of Pakistan returned to the United States in September 1962, Mrs. Kennedy was eager to show him how happy Sardar was in Middleburg. You can see how relaxed and happy they are, simply riding together on the grounds of Glen Ora, with the children's swing set in the background. No pretense.

When Howard sent over the proofs, Mrs. Kennedy was so enamored with the photos that she decided to use one of them as the children's official birthday picture. John would be turning two on November 25, and three days later, Caroline would turn five. It was the only photograph Howard Allen took that was published during Mrs. Kennedy's lifetime.

In 2013, Howard Allen asked Caroline Kennedy for permission to self-publish a book, *Unforgotten Times: Jackie Kennedy's Happy Days in the Virginia Hunt Country*, using some of the treasured photos he took in Middleburg. It is a testament to Jacqueline Kennedy's trust in Howard that Caroline gave her blessing without hesitation.

Long after I was out of Mrs. Kennedy's life, after she no longer received Secret Service protection, Middleburg remained Mrs. Kennedy's happy place. It was one of the few places she could go and be among friends, friends who shared similar interests and who treated her as one of them. Middleburg was the one place where Mrs. Kennedy could almost live a normal life.

12

———

THE SPY
CAMERA

———

ALEXANDRIA, VIRGINIA, 2019

I sat down in the chair behind the desk and pulled open one of the file drawers. It was empty, except for a few house-maintenance files and some oversized manila folders shoved in the back. When I moved out years before, I had removed all the files that contained Secret Service–related issues, so I wasn't expecting to find anything of that nature, but I honestly couldn't remember what I'd stored in there. I pulled out one of the folders and laid it on the desk. On the outside of the folder, I'd written in blue ink: *Italy clippings*. I opened the metal clasp and, sure enough, that's what was inside: dozens of newspaper clippings from Mrs. Kennedy's vacation in Italy the summer of 1962.

I used to always send my mother a postcard from each place we visited. She would cut out every newspaper article that mentioned Mrs. Kennedy's trips and paste them into scrapbooks with the postcards so she could show all our relatives back in North Dakota. When my mother had to be moved into a nursing home, my sister sent me dozens of scrapbooks and boxes filled with newspaper clippings. I guess I'd tucked them away, thinking one day I'd read them.

As I inspected the grainy photographs and scanned the yellowed newspaper stories filled with details I'd long since forgotten, the memories came back like a movie in my mind.

ITALIANS WOULD FACE SHARKS FOR HER was the headline of one article. Dated August 8, 1962, the article noted that Mrs. Kennedy should be warned about the amorous nature of Italian men and their habit of giving audacious compliments to beautiful foreigners. "La Signora Kennedy should not have fear if she will learn that Italians would be ready to face the sharks of the Ravello seas to defend her, but before a beautiful woman they are absolutely incapable of containing their expressions of admiration."

It was true. But it wasn't just men. Everywhere we went, it seemed the entire population stopped everything they would normally be doing to watch Mrs. Kennedy do whatever she was doing. This was the summer of 1962, and by that time, Mrs. Kennedy had begun getting used to her celebrity. She would never understand the fascination people had with her, but when we were out of the country, somehow, she took it more in stride. Up to a point. In Ravello, it really got out of hand.

I was starting to feel overwhelmed with all the stuff that was still in the basement. I truly hadn't realized how much there was.

"Lisa!" I called out. "Can you come here?"

She came walking in from the garage, her hair tousled, her previously clean blouse marred with decades-old dust, carrying a small box in her hands.

"What is it? Did you find something?" she asked.

"I just don't know what to keep and what to throw away. I have no idea why I saved all these newspaper clippings from our trip to Ravello in 1962."

"Let me see," Lisa said.

She handled the brittle newspaper like it was fragile china, carefully taking out one page after another and placing them on the desk.

Beneath all the newspaper clippings, there was a stack of loose, eight-by-ten glossy black-and-white photographs. "Oh wow," she gasped. "I've never seen these photos anywhere before. Why do you have them?"

The first two on top of the pile were candid close-up shots of Mrs. Kennedy sitting at a table next to Caroline, eating spaghetti.

Mrs. Kennedy and Caroline sharing a plate of spaghetti on the outdoor terrace of the beach house at Conca dei Marini during our August 1962 trip to Ravello, Italy.

"Benno must have taken these," I said. "Graziani. He's the only photographer who would have had that kind of access because he was staying at the villa. I guess he gave them to me. But what do I do with them? Keep or toss?"

"Oh my God," Lisa said. "Keep. Keep. Keep!"

I started flipping through the photos. "Here's one," I said. "She's coming out of a shop eating gelato. Looks like chocolate. That's Paul Landis on the left. He was there with Caroline. And that's one of the Italian security guys on the right, obviously glaring at the photographer."

"So what was her reaction to all the people and photographers following her all the time?" Lisa asked.

"You can see she's got a little smirk on her face in this one," I pointed out. "Probably because Landis is confronting someone. She thought that was kind of funny."

I picked up another photo. "Here's a picture of Mrs. Kennedy coming out of church in Ravello. We're about to walk up the steps to her villa and I'm leading the way. Right next to her is the mayor of Ravello, and a few Italian security officers behind her. I would walk in front, spreading my arms, motioning to the people to clear a path for us, and they would. They were all very nice people. They just wanted to be as close to Mrs. Kennedy as possible. And she was very receptive to it, within reason. She liked her space. But I think she was flattered by the attention. You can see it in her eyes."

"In these other photographs," I added, showing her the rest of them, "taken up at the beach house having lunch after a swim with Caroline, you can see how much more relaxed she is."

"I love these," Lisa said. "She's just a mother with her daughter on her lap, eating spaghetti."

"Yes, that was really what was most important to her. Being a good mother," I said.

"Oh, and look what I found in the trunk," Lisa said as she handed me a small black leather case. "I thought it was a pocketknife. But obviously not. What is this?"

I rolled the case over in my hands. I hadn't thought about this in years. "I'll tell you what this is," I said. I tried to suppress my smile as I looked to see Lisa's reaction. "It's a camera."

"What?" She looked at me, her eyes opening wide. "Like the spy camera Mrs. Kennedy had in India?"

"Right," I said. "That's exactly what it is."

"And this other little box was packed in with it," she said. "I was just about to open it when you called me."

As she handed me the box and I read the name on the address label, a shiver ran through me.

Mark Shaw
142 East 30th Street
New York, New York
From: Minox processing laboratories

I lifted the lid off the box. Inside was an envelope stuffed with a stack of small square black-and-white photographs.

"Well, I'll be damned," I said. "These are from Ravello. I imagine you're going to want to keep these."

I looked at each photograph and handed them to Lisa, one by one.

"You took these?" she whispered.

"I did. I had completely forgotten about them. See this one," I said, pointing, "that's on board the *Agneta*, Gianni Agnelli's yacht. We're under sail. It looks like Mrs. Kennedy caught me taking the picture. You can see the Amalfi coast in the background.

"I was the only agent on board. I'd go up on the bow and just try to stay out of the way. Stay out of earshot of their conversations so Mrs. Kennedy could feel like she had privacy and forget I was even there."

Top: One of the photos I took aboard the *Agneta* with my spy camera during our trip to Ravello, Italy. That's Mrs. Kennedy in the scarf and sunglasses talking to Mrs. Agnelli.

Bottom: Mrs. Kennedy sitting on the back of the Riva. She had obviously caught me taking this photo from aboard Gianni Agnelli's yacht *Agneta*. There was so much activity— they were always coming and going from the yacht to the beach house to the villa. That little Riva was our private water taxi. Everyone loved it.

"Where did you get the camera? Did all the agents have these?"

"No, no. After we came back from India and Pakistan, when I'd seen Mrs. Kennedy with that little camera, I called Mark Shaw and asked him if he could get me one. So when we went to Ravello, that was the first time I used it."

"Was it to spy on Mrs. Kennedy?" Lisa asked.

"No, no. For God's sake, no. See here?" I pointed to one of the pictures of three young men smiling, wearing T-shirts with AGNETA embroidered on them. "These were the crew members on Gianni Agnelli's yacht, the *Agneta*. They saw me using the camera one day and I told them I wanted to take their photo for Mrs. Kennedy's album. But it was really just to have a picture of the crew so in case anything happened, I had a photograph to be able to identify them. I went around and took pictures of all the staff who were helping us, just because you never know who is going to try to do something or take advantage of the situation of being in close proximity to her."

"Did she know you had the camera?" Lisa asked.

"Oh, I'm sure she did. She was smart and intuitive. She knew what was going on."

"Oh my God! Look at this one!" Lisa exclaimed as she picked up a photo at the bottom of the box. It was larger, five by seven, and unlike all the others, this one was in color. "That's you! And Toby! Look how handsome you are!"

Agent Toby Chandler and I were bare-chested, in swim trunks, casually sitting on the bow of a boat, anchored off the rocky shore near Conca dei Marini, Italy. Toby had a stern look on his face, I was laughing, and behind us, two Italian security guys were hamming it up for the photographer.

"I was thirty years old then," I reminded her.

"It's so rare to see a picture of you laughing," Lisa said.

It seemed like another lifetime. And yet I could feel the boat rocking gently, the hot August sun on my back. And I could see that glimmer in Mrs. Kennedy's eyes.

Agent Toby Chandler, me, and two Italian security guys on one of the security boats we used on the Amalfi coast during our trip to Ravello, Italy.

13

———

RAVELLO

———

1962

T he two-week trip to Italy in August 1962 was meant to be purely a vacation for Mrs. Kennedy and Caroline, who was four at the time. No official visits or state dinners. Just a relaxing seaside holiday with family and close friends.

Along with Stash and Lee Radziwill and their young son, Tony, Mrs. Kennedy had invited her friend Benno Graziani; his wife, Nicole; and Mark Shaw and his wife, singer Pat Suzuki. They had rented a villa in the relatively unknown town of Ravello, a hidden treasure of a village perched twelve hundred feet above the Mediterranean Sea on the Amalfi coast. The nine-hundred-year-old Villa Episcopio was surrounded by high stone walls, had spectacular views of the dramatic coastline, and provided the privacy Mrs. Kennedy needed, while still being centrally located so she could wander through the maze of cobblestone streets lined with gelato shops, outdoor cafés, and family-owned trattorias.

They'd also rented a "beach house" in Conca dei Marini, which was about a fifteen-minute drive down the narrow, winding road, etched into the cliffs, and had direct access to the water for swimming and waterskiing.

I was still Mrs. Kennedy's only full-time Secret Service Agent, since Jeffries had left back in March, so once again, I got to pick a small team of agents to assist. Toby Chandler and Paul Rundle would help with Mrs. Kennedy's protection and logistics, while Paul Landis and Bob Foster were responsible for Caroline. Other than the agents and Mrs. Kennedy's personal maid, Provi, there was no other staff.

"You can handle everything, Mr. Hill," Mrs. Kennedy had told me before we left. "I don't need a social secretary or press person on a little trip like this."

Every day was an adventure. There was no schedule, no plan. Just how Mrs. Kennedy liked to operate. It made it a bit trickier from my point of view, but we managed. The "beach house" in Conca dei Marini, it turned out, was more like a little bungalow perched precariously into the rocky cliff, with a steep set of stairs leading down to a small cement landing with a ladder to get in and out of the water. The most efficient way to get there from Ravello, however, was to drive down to Amalfi and go by boat. We had a sleek Riva motorboat at our disposal and a couple of umbrella-topped open-air Fiat vehicles for traveling up and down the steep, curvy roads. Fortunately, we had local drivers who knew each hairpin turn and a boat captain who was a master at navigating the sometimes choppy waters.

Opposite left: Mrs. Kennedy was gracious to everyone, always smiling when a photographer would call out her name because she knew if she scowled, that would be the picture in the paper. Lee Radziwill, Mrs. Kennedy, and Caroline (who was just getting used to this constant attention from the public), and that's me looking up with disdain at someone on a balcony or in a window above us. August 1962, Ravello, Italy.

Opposite right: The landing at Conca dei Marini with steps leading up to the "beach house." Agent Paul Landis is in the water with Caroline (in the inflatable duck); I'm glaring at the photographer. Mrs. Kennedy is holding her nephew Tony, who has obviously had an accident requiring a bandage on his face. The man in the white T-shirt is the Italian caretaker of the beach house, who helped us immensely.

Top: It was a tough job, but somebody had to do it. That's me on the back of the Riva in black, with (from left to right) the wonderful Italian caretaker of the beach house who assisted us with everything, Nicole Graziani, Lee and Stash Radziwill, Mrs. Kennedy (in pink), and Benno Graziani standing taking photos.

Bottom: Everyone loved riding around Ravello, Amalfi, and Positano in the open-air Fiats. Left to right: Nicole Graziani, Lee Radziwill with her son, Tony, Mrs. Kennedy holding Caroline, and me in the front.

Mrs. Kennedy finally agreed to give the paparazzi a photo session: Benno Graziani holding his camera, Mrs. Kennedy with a scowling Caroline and Tony Radziwill, Agent Paul Rundle, and the hardworking Italian caretaker of the Conca dei Marini beach house.

The other agents and I communicated with two-way radios, using our Secret Service code names. Mrs. Kennedy was Lace and Caroline was Lyric. All the agents who were permanently assigned to members of the president's family were given names that began with the letter *D*. We didn't choose our own names, they were assigned by our supervisors, and they tried to come up with a word that was somehow descriptive of the person so you could remember it easily. Agent Bob Foster was Dresser because he was fastidious about his clothes; Paul Landis was Debut because he was the youngest agent on the detail. They called me Dazzle. I have no idea how they came up that one, but it stuck and remained my name for my entire career.

The local townspeople were so excited for Mrs. Kennedy's visit that they had hung welcome banners in Ravello's piazza and on the cliff by the stairs near the beach house. Crowds gathered wherever Mrs. Kennedy went, calling out: *"Ciao, Jacqueline!" "Welcome to Ravello!" "Italy loves you!"*

She would wave and smile, soaking in the authentic Italian hospitality. The locals were wonderful. It was the paparazzi that created all the problems. Mrs. Kennedy simply wanted to have a fun, normal, relaxing vacation, but the Italian paparazzi just wouldn't leave her alone. I finally convinced her that the best way to deal with them was to agree to pose so they'd get one good picture. After that, if they persisted, we could push harder to keep them away.

A few days into the trip, Gianni Agnelli—the owner of Fiat—and his wife, Marella, sailed in on their magnificent yacht *Agneta*. The Agnellis were friends of Mrs. Kennedy's, and they graciously offered to allow her to use the yacht as much as she wanted. We realized it was much easier to keep the press away when we'd go sailing off to some unknown destination and anchor offshore so she could swim and waterski.

When we were sailing on the *Agneta*, I would usually stay up on the bow, out of the way, so Mrs. Kennedy could enjoy the time with her friends. Here are Marella Agnelli, Benno Graziani, Pat Suzuki (seated in scarf), Mrs. Kennedy (holding a camera), Nicole Graziani, a crew member standing, Gianni Agnelli at the helm, and Mark Shaw (partially obstructed) holding a camera.

Top: I was usually the only agent on the yacht. I communicated with the other agents, who were onshore and in motorboats, with a Motorola walkie-talkie.

Bottom: Mrs. Kennedy relied on me to handle everything. Here she is in one of the powerboats probably telling me about some change of plans. That's me, in the jazzy swim trunks, listening intently to her instructions, alongside two of the crew members in their matching uniforms.

Top: Much as she tried to blend in as just another tourist, it was almost impossible. Two agents are in the water with Mrs. Kennedy as she pushes Caroline and her nephew Tony on a raft amid the rowboats filled with curious locals and paparazzi.

Bottom: Mrs. Kennedy loved to waterski and would do it at any available opportunity. In Ravello, she caused a stir when she took four-year-old Caroline out waterskiing with her, neither one of them wearing a life jacket. I didn't worry because I knew what an excellent water-skier Mrs. Kennedy was and that Caroline, even at that young age, was a strong swimmer.

We used the Riva like a taxi to transfer Mrs. Kennedy, the kids, and everyone else from the Amalfi pier to Conca dei Marini, out to the *Agneta*, and back again. Typically, we'd end up back at the beach house, late in the afternoon, everyone sunburned and tired. Up the steep steps we'd go, and as you got closer to the house, the heavenly smell of olive oil and garlic would bathe your senses. Mrs. Kennedy and her friends would gather around the outdoor table as the caretaker and his wife served steaming bowls of pasta mixed with freshly caught squid or basil and tomatoes straight from the garden.

Left: Caroline and Mrs. Kennedy just out of the water after a swim.

Opposite right: In order to get to the beach house at Conca dei Marini, we tied the Riva to the dock. It was somewhat precarious to get in and out of the boat, and then you had to walk up a steep set of stairs to get to the house. Here are Lee, Marella Agnelli, Mrs. Kennedy, Stash, and Gianni Agnelli walking up the steps after an afternoon of sailing and waterskiing.

Top: Mrs. Kennedy was so relaxed around her close friends. No makeup, hair wet from an after-swim shower. Left to right: Mrs. Kennedy enjoys time with Marella Agnelli, Benno Graziani, Stash Radziwill, and Gianni Agnelli.

Bottom: While Stash and Nicole Graziani play a board game, Mrs. Kennedy enjoys some quiet time. Next to her there's a stack of photos, which Benno had developed, and she's probably making notes of which ones she wants copies of for herself or to share with friends. She always had a pad with her for taking notes or sketching.

The other agents and I tried to be as unobtrusive as possible to allow Mrs. Kennedy her privacy. Someone would guard the entry of the house, while I usually stayed down on the platform with the boats. Fortunately, the cook always made extra food, which we greatly appreciated.

One afternoon, I somehow managed to step on a sea urchin. Being from North Dakota, I had never had an encounter with these spiny underwater creatures, and at first I had no idea what had hit me—just that I'd stepped on something sharp and it stung like hell. I sucked it up until we got back to Ravello and Mrs. Kennedy was situated in the villa, then limped barefoot up the cobblestone street to the Hotel Palumbo, where the other agents and I were staying. When I walked into the lobby, the man at the front desk saw that I was in pain and asked what was wrong. I pointed to my foot, and before I knew it, I was sitting on a chair while two young women who worked at the hotel were kneeling at my feet. They poured some kind of liquid all over the foot and then proceeded to pull out the tiny spikes with tweezers. There seemed to be some urgency to their actions, and I wondered if perhaps I should have been more concerned than I was. Whatever they did worked and I was much better the following morning.

One day we sailed to Paestum, an ancient Greco-Roman city about forty miles down the coast from Amalfi. One of the *Agneta* crew members rowed us to shore, and then we walked to the site of the ruins. By the time we were ready to go back to the yacht, a few paparazzi had followed us to the shore. The crew member and rowboat were waiting for us, but the sea was rougher than it had been when we arrived, making it a bit treacherous to get into the little boat.

Mrs. Kennedy had no trouble getting in, but the boat was crashing against the rocky shore as the paparazzi were snapping away. I didn't want anyone to get a compromising photo of her, so I yelled out, "Put down your damn cameras and somebody give us a push before we swamp!"

Mrs. Kennedy found it amusing whenever I'd get the least bit ruffled about something, and she thought the whole situation was hilarious.

"Oh, Mr. Hill!" she said, laughing.

Benno Graziani always had his camera at the ready, and he captured that moment perfectly.

Mrs. Kennedy found it amusing whenever I'd get the least bit ruffled about something. I'm yelling at the paparazzi to give us a push before our little rowboat swamps, and she's laughing, thinking it's hilarious.

Even though I wasn't there as a guest or a friend, there's no denying the intimacy that developed between Mrs. Kennedy and me on that trip. It wasn't romantic. But it was beyond friendship. We could communicate with a look or a nod. I could sense when she was uncomfortable or just wanted some extra space from the agents. She knew that I would do whatever she asked—and I would, as long as I could justify it for security reasons. She also knew that anything I requested of her was for her own well-being. All I wanted was for her to be happy and safe.

Opposite: Mrs. Kennedy was so carefree on the trip to Ravello. Walking back to the rowboat from Paestum, someone must have said something funny, which made Mrs. Kennedy turn and laugh, while I'm trying to hide my own amusement. Every day was filled with fun and laughter.

Top: This is how I typically saw Mrs. Kennedy during those three weeks on the Amalfi coast: hair swept up, blowing in the wind, still wet from swimming or waterskiing. She loved being out on the water. But even on a boat, it was difficult to escape the constant intrusion of people wanting to see her.

Bottom: In an effort to blend in, I ditched my normal attire of suit and tie, and used the TWA bag to carry everything I needed, including my gun and all our passports. I tried to make sure Mrs. Kennedy didn't have to worry about anything so she could simply enjoy a fun and relaxing vacation.

Top: I was always concerned when Mrs. Kennedy was getting in and out of the boats. We had a great group of Italian guys working with us, though, who were always willing to help lend a hand.

Bottom: Local paparazzi were everywhere. They would run ahead of us and click away. I tried to give Mrs. Kennedy her space, while still being close enough to see everything that was going on.

Opposite left: Mrs. Kennedy attended Mass each Sunday we were in Ravello, and the crowds would gather in the streets to see her walk by. The people were friendly, but I couldn't let my guard down. You never knew when someone would suddenly lunge at her.

Opposite right: Walking through the ancient stone streets of Ravello with Mrs. Kennedy. My usual Florsheim wingtips looked out of place on the coast of Italy, so Mrs. Kennedy convinced me to buy a pair of handmade Italian loafers.

Mark Shaw had brought an extra camera, which he loaned to Mrs. Kennedy during the trip, and she was having fun taking pictures. It was late one afternoon, as I recall, and the paparazzi had gone away, so we were all a lot more relaxed. The *Agneta* was anchored, and Toby and I were on the security boat when Mrs. Kennedy called out, "Hey, Dazzle!"

She had never called me by my code name before, and it caught me by surprise. I turned, laughing, and there she was, snapping a photo.

Left: There's no denying the intimacy that developed between Mrs. Kennedy and me on the trip to Ravello. It wasn't romantic, but it was beyond friendship. She trusted me implicitly. All I wanted was for her to be happy and safe.

Opposite: Mark Shaw loaned Mrs. Kennedy one of his cameras. Here she is aboard the *Agneta*, balancing the camera in one hand and a cigarette between her fingers of the other. "Hey, Dazzle!" she called out to me.

14

———

THE
SKETCHBOOK

———

ALEXANDRIA, VIRGINIA, 2019

By the time the sun began to set each day in Alexandria, my back would really start hurting—a signal it was time to quit. I wasn't used to moving boxes around and hauling bags of trash. I was nearly eighty-eight years old, and while my mind was reliving life like I was thirty again, my body had no qualms about snapping me back to reality.

It was always a relief to get back to the Willard, where there was no clutter, no boxes or cupboards to sort through. Lisa and I would walk into the suite and both of us would let out an audible sigh. Because we had stayed in this same suite so many times, it really felt like our home away from home. We would get cleaned up and go out to dinner somewhere or sometimes just go down in the elevator to the historic Round Robin bar and have a drink and a couple of appetizers.

On this particular night, though, we were both exceptionally tired, so we decided to stay in and order room service. "Let's have a glass of wine in the living room," I said to Lisa. "I found something today I'd like to show you."

We settled down on the sofa and I pulled a large envelope marked WHITE HOUSE out of my briefcase.

"I found this tucked in the back of my desk drawer," I said, pulling out the contents.

"What is it?" Lisa asked.

"It's Mrs. Kennedy's sketchbook. From when we were on Onassis's yacht in October 1963. And the original manifest list of passengers and crew."

"I just got shivers," Lisa said. "And what's that?" she asked, pointing to the yellow box in my hand.

"Film negatives from that same trip."

October 1963

In October 1963, Mrs. Kennedy was invited to spend ten days cruising the Mediterranean on Aristotle Onassis's yacht *Christina*. Arranged by her sister Lee, the cruise was an attempt to boost Mrs. Kennedy's spirits after the traumatic loss of her newborn baby son. Patrick Bouvier Kennedy was born August 7, six weeks prematurely, and lived just thirty-nine hours. The loss was devastating to President and Mrs. Kennedy, as well as to all of us who were around them.

Everyone hoped some time away would help Mrs. Kennedy through her grieving process. Even President Kennedy supported the trip.

We boarded the 325-foot *Christina* in Glyfada, Greece. Just ten passengers and a crew of forty-eight.

The yacht was as opulent as you can imagine. Solid-gold fixtures in all the bathrooms. Faucets in the shape of dolphins. A spiral staircase with pillars of onyx soaring three levels. A swimming pool on the upper deck that could be quickly drained and transformed into a dance floor with the push of a button. A helicopter with its own landing pad.

The *Christina* anchored at Istanbul. I was one of ten passengers aboard, along with a crew of forty-eight to attend to one's every need. Aristotle Onassis was there, but he spent much of the time barking orders into a telephone from his suite off the bridge. He and Mrs. Kennedy spent very little time together, but he clearly wanted to do everything he could to make this trip enjoyable for her, just two months after the death of her newborn son, Patrick.

Top: I had the passenger list complete with passport numbers and nationality. Note that Aristotle Onassis's nationality is listed as Argentine. As I went around and met each of the forty-eight crew members, I put a check mark next to their names.

Bottom: Aristotle Onassis checks on his guests, who are having an afternoon snack and cocktail. It looks like Mrs. Kennedy is having Campari. With her are Franklin D. Roosevelt Jr. and his wife, Suzanne. Mr. Onassis and I did not get along very well. He tolerated me, but he did not respect the fact that I was there to protect Mrs. Kennedy. He had his own security people, who he thought were much better than any U.S. Secret Service agent.

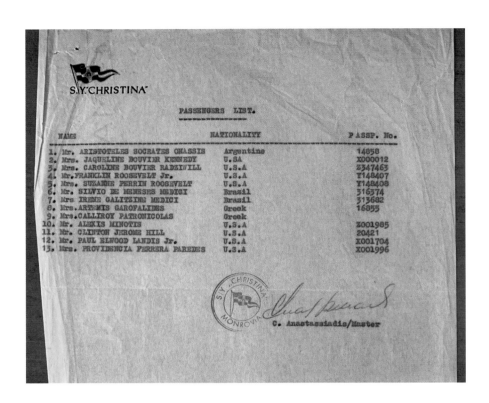

S.Y. CHRISTINA

PASSENGERS LIST.

NAME	NATIONALITY	PASSP. No.
1. Mr. ARISTOTELES SOCRATES ONASSIS	Argentine	14858
2. Mrs. JAQUELINE BOUVIER KENNEDY	U.SA	X000012
3. Mrs. CAROLINE BOUVIER RADZIWILL	U.S.A	Z347463
4. Mr. FRANKLIN ROOSEVELT Jr.	U.S.A	Y148407
5. Mrs. SUZANNE PERRIN ROOSEVELT	U.S.A	Y148408
6. Mr. SILVIO DE MENESES MEDICI	Brazil	516374
7. Mrs IRENE GALITZINE MEDICI	Brazil	313682
8. Mrs. ARTEMIS GAROFALIDES	Greek	16855
9. Mrs. CALLIROY PATRONICOLAS	Greek	
10. Mr. ALEXIS MINOTIS	U.S.A	Z001985
11. Mr. CLINTON JEROME HILL	U.S.A	20421
12. Mr. PAUL ELWOOD LANDIS Jr.	U.S.A	X001704
13. Mrs. PROVIDENCIA FERRERA PAREDES	U.S.A	X001996

C. Anastassiadis/Master

We cruised to Istanbul, then down the coast of Turkey back to Greece, making stops in Crete, Lefkas, and Onassis's private island of Skorpios. The two-week cruise ended with a stop in Delphi before heading back to Athens.

For Mrs. Kennedy, this was a chance to get away from the reminders of the tragic loss of her son and to be out of the public eye. Every stop on the itinerary was unannounced, and while the press followed the ship's every move—and managed to get some coveted photos of her onshore—for the most part, it was very private. She was able to spend time with friends, Lee, and Stash, whom she truly adored. Mr. Onassis spent most of the time in his apartment near the bridge, barking orders on the phone. He made sure she had everything she wanted or needed, but he participated in few of the activities.

Everywhere we traveled, Mrs. Kennedy studied the history of the place so that when she walked through ruins of fortresses or castles, she could imagine what life was like. She wasn't content to just sit on the yacht and look at scenery go by. She wanted to explore the sites like any other tourist. Here I try to remain unobtrusive as she and Lee walk through the Palace of Knossos on Crete.

Top: Agent Paul Landis (right) getting a history lesson about antique jewelry with Lee and Mrs. Kennedy during one of our stops in the Greek islands.

Bottom: There were few tourists at the amphitheater in Delphi, and Mrs. Kennedy loved being able to explore the area without a throng of crowds following her. Some, like the man on the steps in the background, realized who she was and got the unexpected bonus of a photograph of Jacqueline Kennedy to paste into their photo albums.

There were long stretches of time when we were just cruising along, and Mrs. Kennedy would be sitting on a lounge chair on the deck, with the sketch pad and watercolor paint set she had asked me to buy during our stop in Istanbul. She would gaze out at the sea with the picturesque villages dotted along the coast, dipping the paintbrush in water and then in one paint and another, mixing the colors to try to match the azure water as it changed with the light.

One of her favorite gifts to give people was a painting or sketch commemorating a special event they had shared together. Her paintings were typically soft and airy, with a hint of whimsy that depicted her sense of humor.

By the end of the trip, Mrs. Kennedy had really begun to come out of her depression. She was laughing again, and I was hopeful she would be able to move forward with her life. She and President Kennedy had purchased a piece of property in the Middleburg area and had just recently finished completion of the house there, which she was calling Wexford, after the name of the town the Kennedy clan hailed from in Ireland.

She and the president were planning to spend their first weekends there together when we returned, and she was making notes about all the different things she still needed to purchase or move from storage.

A couple of days before we were to return to Athens, she told me she had accepted an invitation from King Hassan of Morocco to attend the celebration of the fortieth day in the life of the king's firstborn son, Prince Mohammed. She had conferred with the president, and all the arrangements were being made for us to fly on the king's private plane from Athens to Marrakesh.

Because of the sudden change of plans, there was a bit of a rush as we were leaving the *Christina*. Even though we were pressed for time, there was something I had to do before we disembarked. Once all of the luggage had been removed and Mrs. Kennedy had departed her suite, I went in to do a final sweep. I did it every time she stayed in a hotel room or even a friend's guesthouse, and especially here on Aristotle Onassis's yacht. I made sure there wasn't anything left in the trash bins—a receipt or napkin with lipstick on it—and went through every drawer, cupboard, and closet to make sure she hadn't accidentally left anything behind. It was in the drawer of one of the nightstands in her stateroom that I found the sketchbook. I stuffed it in my briefcase for safekeeping until we returned to Washington.

Our arrival in Morocco. We flew in the king of Morocco's private plane from Athens to Marrakesh. I am not too pleased when the Moroccan chief of protocol suddenly grabs Mrs. Kennedy's hand to kiss it.

Mrs. Kennedy was in such high spirits after the relaxing cruise that I was concerned this celebration for the king's son might cause her to regress. Prince Mohammed was born August 21, so he was about the same age baby Patrick would have been had he lived. Fortunately, from the moment we landed in Marrakesh, there were so many planned activities that we were going from one event to another. She was kept so busy and occupied, there wasn't much time for her to be alone and think. While I had at first been concerned about this trip, it turned out that traveling to a new and exotic country, surrounded by people she trusted and with whom she felt comfortable, was therapeutic.

The previous March, President and Mrs. Kennedy had hosted King Hassan, who was accompanied by his brother, Moulay Abdallah, and sister Lalla Nuzha, with a state dinner at the White House. The three siblings were close in age to Mrs. Kennedy, and she could converse easily with them in both French and English, so they had struck up a fond rapport.

As it turned out, while we were in Morocco, the king was dealing with a breakout war with Algeria, so the last night of our visit, his brother Moulay Abdallah hosted the dinner for Mrs. Kennedy.

It was a very festive atmosphere, with traditional dancers, Moroccan drums, and some percussion instruments that Mrs. Kennedy found intriguing.

After dinner, they passed around tea and trays of desserts.

"What are these?" I asked, as I picked up one of the round confectionary treats off a tray and took a bite.

"*Mahjoun*. Moroccan specialty," the server answered.

Everyone was laughing and dancing, and Mrs. Kennedy was partaking in all the fun. It had been a long time since I'd seen Mrs. Kennedy really let her guard down like that. I too felt a lot more relaxed. *Mahjoun*, it turned out, was the Moroccan version of hash brownies.

They had an official Moroccan photographer there, which was fine, but by the end of the evening I realized there could be some pictures that might not be flattering to Mrs. Kennedy. I explained to the photographer that this was meant to be a purely private visit for Mrs. Kennedy and that I would need to take his film so we could preview the photographs.

The U.S. Secret Service had such an impeccable reputation and was regarded so highly all over the world that there was no question about handing over the film to me.

When we returned to Washington, I asked Cecil Stoughton, the White House photographer, to develop the film. He printed the photographs and returned the negatives to me.

I looked at the photos, and while there were some good mementos of that wild night, there were indeed some unflattering pictures of Mrs. Kennedy. I was sure glad I had gotten the negatives. I slipped all the photographs into an envelope and took them to her, along with the sketchbook I had retrieved.

"Mrs. Kennedy, I took the film from the photographer that last night in Morocco, and here are the photographs. No one else has seen them."

"Oh, thank you, Mr. Hill. That was such a fun evening. I hope you enjoyed it as much as I did!"

"Those crazy Moroccans." I laughed. "Oh, and I forgot to give this to you," I said, handing her the sketchbook. "I found it in your stateroom just as we were leaving the *Christina*."

She flipped through the pages. "Oh, I already took everything out of this that I needed. These are just my sketches and paint drafts. You can throw it away."

"Okay," I said. I stuck it back in my briefcase, intending to dispose of it properly.

A few of the photos from the party in Marrakesh hosted by King Hassan's brother, Moulay Abdallah (in the striped djellaba).

Bottom: That's me in the tuxedo walking behind Lee, Mrs. Kennedy, and Moulay Abdallah.

Mrs. Kennedy, Moulay Abdallah, and Lee Radziwill departing the party by car.

The Willard
Washington, D.C., 2019

"These pictures from Morocco are incredible," Lisa said. "But I'm dying to see what's in that sketchbook."

"There's really not that much in it," I said. "Go ahead. Take a look." The first page was a whimsical pencil sketch of the *Christina* in the sea with the Greek flag on her stern. Two dolphins, two fish, and a serpent appeared to be leaping out of the water next to the yacht, while two figures stood on the shore in the left lower corner, waving.

The next page was watercolor brush strokes in various shades of aqua, turquoise, and mermaid green—the colors of the Mediterranean. With darker navy blue, she had painted: *Au revoir, Ari* and *Merci.*

"This looks like she was blending colors to create that intense color of the sea along the Greek coast," Lisa said.

"She probably painted a version of the pencil sketch of the *Christina* with her and Lee waving good-bye to give Mr. Onassis as a thank-you gift," I explained. "She liked to give personal gifts like that. She knew it meant more than anything she could buy."

The next page had a simple, childlike sketch of a helicopter surrounded by splashes of paint in various blues, white, and red.

"John loved helicopters," I said. "I would guess this was a sketch for a painting she did for him as a gift when she returned, perhaps to tell him about the helicopter that landed on the yacht."

There were a few other pages with dabs of paint and then another filled with her handwritten notes regarding furnishings for the house in Wexford. She had written a note to remind herself to ask about wiring for the Victrola and made lists of specific items she wanted in various rooms: red lamps and a Mount Vernon painting in the library; Jack's stool and hanging bookcase; a red stripe Louis XVI chair for her dressing room.

"Just seeing these sketches and notes gives me an even better sense of what she was really like," Lisa said.

"This is what she was doing while she was on the yacht in Greece," I said. "Looking forward to putting the finishing touches on their new home, Wexford. She wanted to make it cozy and comfortable—a place she and her husband and the children would enjoy going to for weekends away from Washington. A private retreat."

I closed the sketchbook and said, "So, what do I do with this? I mean, look at all this crap I've got that I don't know what to do with."

"Just for the record, I don't think any of it is crap," Lisa said. "A lot of people would say it's historic. But I have another question. It's about Onassis."

"I never understood that relationship," I said.

"I know you didn't like him, but do you think that trip on the *Christina* gave her a taste of privacy that she'd never had before? I mean, you've always said that she craved privacy."

"I don't think she ever thought about Onassis again until June 6, 1968. When Bobby was killed, the whole game changed."

"So when she returned to Washington after Morocco, there was no sense of anything romantic with Onassis?"

"None whatsoever. When we got back to Washington, she was rejuvenated. The death of Patrick had brought her and President Kennedy closer together than ever before, and now she was in the mindset of four more years in the White House with Wexford as their weekend retreat.

"All of us around them felt this sense of relief, in a way. The next two weekends we went to Wexford, and it really felt like we'd been through the worst and come out of it."

15

WEXFORD

OCTOBER 1963

T he first weekend after we returned from Morocco we went to Wexford. On the short helicopter ride from the White House to Atoka, the little community in Fauquier County in which the house was located, Mrs. Kennedy was more talkative than usual. She was so happy to be home with her family. The house sat on top of a hill with sweeping views of the countryside, and there was a large flat area for the helicopter to land just below it.

Looking out the window of Marine One, as we circled in for touchdown, Mrs. Kennedy turned to the president and said, "Isn't it just perfect, Jack?" She was so proud of the house and could hardly wait to spend time there, the whole family together, just like she'd imagined throughout the past year as she was designing it.

While the rest of the staff and I unloaded suitcases and boxes from the helicopter into the station wagon one of the agents had brought around, Mrs. Kennedy grabbed the hands of her children and started marching up the hill toward the house, with Maud Shaw, the children's nanny, following behind.

"We can take you in the car, Mrs. Kennedy," I called out to her. It wasn't very far, but it was somewhat of a steep incline.

She barely turned her head to look back, as if she couldn't take her eyes off the house. "Oh, thank you, Mr. Hill, but the children and I will walk."

She was like a little girl with a new dollhouse. A place she'd decorated in her own taste and where she could move things around without having to worry about how the public would react to every little decision; a place designed specifically for her family and how they lived, with meeting areas for the president, quiet nooks for Mrs. Kennedy to read, write letters, or paint; large living and dining rooms for entertaining friends. She'd even incorporated special areas in which the cooks and housekeepers could sit down and relax. Large windows let in plenty of light and offered bucolic views of the surrounding countryside, and yet, the way the house was situated, it provided complete privacy. Unless you knew exactly where to turn off the road in Atoka, you wouldn't even know it was there. A long driveway tucked in between tall trees led to the house, and planted in the soil next to the entry path was a small black wrought-iron sign on which was embossed: THE JOHN F. KENNEDYS. It struck me as funny, that sign. It was the kind of placard you'd see at the end of a driveway in an ordinary suburban neighborhood like where I lived. I think for her, for Mrs. Kennedy, it was an emblem of the normalcy she craved.

She had a swing set installed on the back patio so the president could sit in a chair nearby to watch and interact with John and Caroline as they swung and climbed. And stuck into the lawn were two spring-loaded riding toys like you'd see in a public playground: a little donkey, the symbol of the Democratic Party; and an airplane, so John could pretend to be a pilot. The children would bounce around for what seemed like hours, as the president fed their imaginations with questions and encouragement.

The main purpose of the property, from Mrs. Kennedy's point of view, of course, was that it had acres and acres for riding. That fall, Caroline was not yet six years old, but she'd become such an accomplished rider that she could trot and even gallop across the meadow all by herself.

It's bittersweet when I think back on those weekends. So many great memories. So much hope. And then, suddenly, it was gone.

Above: President Kennedy loved the freedom of being able to drive around in the golf cart. He's showing his friend Lem Billings around their newly finished home, Wexford, with Mrs. Kennedy and John, October 27, 1963.

Opposite: October 27, 1963: President and Mrs. Kennedy relaxing on the terrace at Wexford—one of the few times they were there together. In front of Mrs. Kennedy is Clipper—a German shepherd that was a gift from her father-in-law.

Above: October 27, 1963. The last time the family attended Mass together was in Middleburg at the recently completed St. Stephen's Catholic Church.

Opposite: November 10, 1963: *Washington Post* editor Ben Bradlee, his wife, Tony Bradlee, and President Kennedy sitting on the terrace wall at Wexford. Mrs. Kennedy is riding Rufus. They are watching friend Paul Fout (not in photo) training Mrs. Kennedy's horse Sardar to jump.

Top: President Kennedy in deep conversation with John on the patio at Wexford as Caroline plays on the swing set.

Bottom: Mrs. Kennedy joins John as he plays Army soldier. They had set up an Army tent for him, and nanny Maud Shaw (in background) played his nurse. That's Clipper in the foreground.

Top: November 10, 1963: Tony Bradlee laughs as President Kennedy is licked by Caroline's pony Leprechaun. Mrs. Kennedy had stuck some sugar cubes in the president's pockets and the pony wouldn't leave him alone. Mrs. Kennedy was off to the side laughing mischievously. It was one of the funniest presidential moments I've ever witnessed.

Bottom: They were so happy to be able to relax with friends at Wexford. Here are Ben and Tony Bradlee, Mrs. Kennedy, Clipper the German shepherd, President Kennedy, and Paul Fout. Mrs. Kennedy had so much hope for their future life together. Twelve days later everything shattered.

Alexandria, 2019

It had been six days since we first arrived, and when I looked around the nearly empty house, I was amazed at the progress we'd made. What had at first felt overwhelming had now become an all-out mission to get everything out so I could put the house on the market.

There was a dumpster in the driveway that was now nearly filled to the brim with old mattresses, furniture that I thought was still in pretty darn good condition but that all the consignment stores informed me was not the kind of stuff people wanted to buy these days, and mounds of other household goods that had outlived their useful life. Lisa and I had set aside all the photos and presidential memorabilia that she'd convinced me to keep so we could ship it to California and figure out what to do with it.

We had found several boxes that contained nothing but newspapers, clippings, and magazines about the assassination, and nearly every book that had been written analyzing what had happened. I had read everything, more than once, and kept it. I had spent years in the basement, torturing myself by reading what others wrote. The images and sounds of November 22, 1963, and the three days that followed are seared into my mind.

It wasn't until Lisa came into my life, by some miracle, and started asking questions—not just about that day, but all that came before, and after. We first met in August 2009, when I agreed to let her interview me for a book she was writing with Jerry Blaine, a former Secret Service agent whom I had worked with during the Kennedy administration. I had never spoken about the assassination to anyone outside the Warren Commission, but Lisa got me to open up. She was genuinely interested. I began to trust her, and the more time we spent together, the more I revealed. I had sworn I would never write a book, but she convinced me my stories were historic and that others might find them interesting too. Over the previous ten years we had written three books together and I had become comfortable speaking publicly about the history I had witnessed. There's no doubt the writing and speaking had been cathartic for me. By this point, I had told her almost everything. Almost.

The one thing that kept creeping into my mind was the daily diary Lisa had found. I hadn't opened it because I wasn't sure how it was going to affect me.

I hadn't told her yet, but I had also set aside a file folder that contained information about something I'd never shared with anyone. I'd found it tucked in the back of one of the file drawers in my old desk.

I'm not sure why I hadn't burned it with all my other sensitive information, but when I saw the file labeled FOR CHIEF'S EYES ONLY!, the mere thought of what it contained caused my body to stiffen, and the sickening, blood-draining feelings returned as if it were that black December night, half a century ago. I had come so far these past ten years. Writing and talking about the assassination had literally brought me back to life after decades of living in my emotional prison. But when I saw the diary and that file—that damn file!—I realized there were still things buried deep inside me that needed to be released.

I went upstairs and found Lisa tying up yet another garbage bag of junk to haul out to the dumpster.

"Lisa," I said. "Let's take a break. Let's go back to the Willard and get cleaned up. I think you're right: I need to talk about 1964. But first, there's something else I need to tell you."

16

———

THE PALM
BEACH
INCIDENT

———

DECEMBER 1963

December 1963 was exceptionally difficult. Excruciating. The new president, Lyndon B. Johnson, had allowed Mrs. Kennedy to take her time moving out of the White House and, because of this unprecedented situation, had requested that Congress pass legislation for the Secret Service to provide protection for Mrs. Kennedy and the children for two years.

Our small team of agents had taken Mrs. Kennedy, John, and Caroline to Hyannis Port for Thanksgiving, and upon our return to Washington, Chief James J. Rowley called me into his office. It's one of those conversations I'll never forget.

"Clint, President Johnson spoke with Mrs. Kennedy and told her she could have any agents she wanted."

A lump filled my throat. I had no idea what he was going to say. Perhaps she wanted a change. Maybe seeing me day in and day out would be a constant reminder of what happened in Dallas. I couldn't imagine not being with her, but in terms of my career, the best option was to be reassigned to the President's Detail. That's where the action was. The primary reason most people wanted to be in the Service was to be protecting the president. It wasn't my decision, though. It was between Mrs. Kennedy and my supervisors.

December 6, 1963:
Mrs. Kennedy and
the children move
out of the White
House. Mr. and
Mrs. Averell
Harriman
generously offered
to let the family
stay in their
residence, as long
as needed, at
3038 N Street NW
in Georgetown.
Mrs. Kennedy puts
on a brave face
as she walks with
Caroline into their
new temporary
home.

Left: John was really too young to understand what was going on. He kept asking for his daddy, and it was just so hard on the agents, particularly Bob Foster, who was with him most of the time. Here Agent Foster is trying to hurry John inside so the photographers can't get any more pictures. But John is insistent: "No, Mr. Foster, I want my flag. I need to carry my flag." So I grabbed his flag out of the back seat and handed it to him, just in time for the photographer to snap this poignant photo.

Right: Ethel and Bobby Kennedy had come to make sure Mrs. Kennedy was settled in. "Thank you," she said as they were leaving. "Don't worry, I'll be fine."

Mrs. Kennedy was concerned that John, who was just three years old, would forget his father's conversations and personality, so she asked Dave Powers—one of President Kennedy's closest friends—to come to the residence as often as possible to talk with John. Dave spoke with that same distinctive Boston Irish accent that President Kennedy had, and he always had a new story to tell young John that would get him giggling. He would drop by on a regular basis around lunchtime, and Mrs. Kennedy was so pleased to see the relationship between the two.

"She didn't hesitate," he continued. "She wants Bob Foster, Lynn Meredith, and Tom Wells to stay with the children."

I nodded. *That* will *be best for John and Caroline.*

"And for herself," Rowley continued, "she said there was no choice to be made at all. She wants Paul Landis and Clint Hill."

I swallowed hard. A jumble of emotions went through me. I should have been disappointed. Protecting a former first lady was a dead-end job. But instead, I felt a sense of relief. No one could ever know her like I did. To be able to anticipate her spontaneity, to allow her space when she wanted it, and to move in close when she was anxious. All she had to do was look at me and I knew what she needed. But our world had crashed in around us, and what had been an effortless dance was now marred by unspeakable pain. Still, I didn't trust anyone else to protect her.

"Thank you, Mr. Rowley," I said. "I think that will be best for her and the children."

"It's temporary, Clint," he added. "At most it will be two years, but let's see how it goes."

Mrs. Kennedy and the children moved out of the White House on December 6. Averell Harriman, a former ambassador and now an official in the State Department, and his wife had offered their residence in Georgetown to her and the children until she could find a suitable new home in the D.C. area. We went back and forth to Wexford a couple of times, but the memories of those wonderful weekends in October were so fresh and haunting, it was almost unbearable for any of us to be there.

The week before Christmas, we flew to Palm Beach, as we had for the three previous years, and while the president's father and much of the rest of the family were there, there was no *Honey Fitz* to take out for a lunchtime cruise, no laughter around the swimming pool, and just the small group of agents on the Kennedy Protective Detail: Paul Landis and me with JBK; Bob Foster, Lynn Meredith, and Tommy Wells with the kids.

Guilt and anguish consumed me. I was barely holding it together. The evening of December 29, 1963, while Paul Landis was on duty at the residence, I headed over to the Palm Beach Athletic Club. I sat alone at the bar, and all I could think about was Dallas. It was like a movie playing over and over in my mind. I was running as fast as I could, my arms reaching for the handholds on the trunk, but it was like my legs were in quicksand. Mrs. Kennedy climbing out of the back seat, her porcelain skin spattered with blood and brain matter, her terrified eyes looking but not seeing me, like I wasn't there.

And now, day after day, watching her try to pick up the pieces of her life, I felt helpless. Useless. The one thing she wanted I couldn't give her. She and her husband had been at the pinnacle of their lives, and in the span of six seconds, everything shattered. The husband and father that we had the responsibility to protect was dead. We had failed.

Six-year-old Caroline would wrap her arms around her mother's neck and try to console her while John, at three, was too young to truly understand. All the adults they relied on for solidity, for answers and guidance, were despondent. There was no more laughter, only tears, and an overwhelming sense of despair. It had to have been confusing—and scary—for the children.

The days were interminable. I yearned for nighttime so I could escape with sleep, but if I was lucky enough to fall asleep, I was tortured with the replaying of that same awful movie. Waking up was a blessing and a curse. It wasn't getting better. Every day was worse than the one before, and I could not imagine a time when anyone would ever smile again. Least of all me.

I finished one last swig of my drink and gently placed the glass down on the bar. The bartender had his back to me, so as I stood up, I pulled some bills out of my wallet and stuck them under the glass.

I walked outside and headed toward the water. It was nearly sunset, close to high tide, and on this cool December evening, the narrow stretch of sand was deserted. The waves were crashing onto the shore, the wind blowing in my face, as I took one step after another, fully clothed, into the ocean.

Tears streamed down my cheeks, and as the cold water enveloped my legs, and then my chest, and up to my shoulders, the tears turned to sobs. I wanted the water to swallow me up, but the force of the waves slammed me back against the bulkhead and my shoes sunk into the sandy bottom, like wet cement. My chest heaved as I pounded the bulkhead with my fists, sobbing.

Over the roar of the raging ocean, I heard someone calling my name, and the next thing I knew, a Palm Beach police officer—a motorcycle cop we worked with regularly—was dragging me back out of the water.

The confidential memorandum that was sent to Secret Service Chief Rowley included the police officer's detailed account of the incident along with a description of the interview the SAIC of the Miami Field Office had with me the following morning. In part, it read:

I found SA Hill at the time of the interview at approximately 10:00 A.M. December 30, 1963, was sober and displayed absolutely no evidence that he had been drinking. He was, as always, alert, intelligent, and displayed no evidence of a mental breakdown. However, I did note that he exhibits all of the manifestations, in my opinion, of a person who is on the verge of a nervous mental breakdown. He is struggling to control his emotions and his body is crying out for relief. This man must be given a rest or both the Service and he will suffer the consequences.

SA Hill stated that he would take leave, as he had had no leave for four years, and probably visit his mother, and that he realized he had to "unwind." During the interview SA Hill's only concern was for the welfare of Mrs. Kennedy and her children, and his dedication to his duties is an inspiration.

For some reason, I kept that report. I have never revealed what happened that night in Palm Beach to anyone, and frankly, it is still difficult for me to admit. I suppose I could have just thrown it into the shredder and no one would have ever known. It would have been one more secret to take to my grave. But somehow, there is a sense of freedom in no longer keeping that darkness to myself. People will judge me, I'm sure. But no one—*no one*—has ever walked in my shoes.

In hindsight, there is no doubt I was suffering from what is now known as post-traumatic stress disorder, or PTSD. I'm sure Mrs. Kennedy, along with everyone else in the presidential limousine and in the follow-up car—the other Secret Service agents, Governor and Mrs. Connally, Dave Powers, and Ken O'Donnell—were all suffering the same mental distress as I was. But none of us talked about it—certainly not with each other. There was no counseling. We were each in our own private torture chamber.

That police officer had saved my life. He made me realize it took a lot more courage to stay than to pick my own time to leave. I had responsibilities for my own family. What good would it do to leave my two sons fatherless?

And what kind of man would I be to abandon Mrs. Kennedy when she had specifically requested me to stay? She was struggling to hold it together for her children.

The least I could do was pretend to be strong and help her try to find some semblance of purpose in whatever her life was going to look like in the aftermath of this cruel nightmare.

17

—————

1964

—————

The morning of January 5, as we were getting ready to depart Palm Beach, I asked Mrs. Kennedy if I could speak with her privately. She had gotten some sun over the past eighteen days, so that her skin was subtly bronzed, but her eyes were still clouded with desolation.

"You had suggested I take some time off," I said. I found myself struggling to get the words out, as my gaze focused on the patterned rug beneath my feet. It wasn't comfortable for me to ask for favors.

"Yes," she said softly. "I think it would be beneficial to you to spend some time with your family. You've given so much of yourself to me and the children. Putting our needs above everything else."

I nodded. "Thank you, Mrs. Kennedy. I suppose when we return to Washington, it's probably as good a time as any. I've made arrangements for Agent Meredith to be in charge, and of course Mr. Landis will be able to handle anything you might need."

I don't know if anyone ever told her what happened that night in Palm Beach, but I really don't think so. The report was filed away and never brought up again.

Agent Landis and I got Mrs. Kennedy and the children settled into the Harriman house in Georgetown, and then I went home to my two-bedroom apartment in Alexandria. This was the fourth year in a row I'd been away over Christmas and New Year's. I took a few days off, but it did little good. I was a stranger in my own home. For the past three years, I had been gone 90 percent of the time; I'd spent more days and nights with Mrs. Kennedy than with my own wife and children. It was the requirement of my job, but it certainly was not a good recipe for a healthy marriage or family life. Many of the agents had requested transfers from the White House Detail in the fall of 1963 for that very reason. With 1964 being a campaign year, the time away from home was going to increase exponentially, and some agents' wives had threatened divorce if their husbands didn't transfer to a field office where investigations were the priority and the hours were much closer to a normal nine-to-five job. But for me, after several days at home, I realized my job was the only thing that was going to keep me sane. The feelings of guilt were only magnified when I was at home. It wasn't fair that my children still had their father and Caroline and John didn't. It wasn't fair that I should take a "break," when Mrs. Kennedy would be a widow for the rest of her life. Every time she walked out the door, she was back in the public eye, people hounding her. Gawking. The least I could do was try to protect her from the press and find ways for her to do things she wanted to do as privately as possible, just as I'd always done.

The police had cordoned off an area of the street in front of the Harriman house at 3038 N Street NW in Georgetown, and we had an agent posted outside the front door. Several groups of people were gathered across the street, cameras in hand, like vultures, hoping to catch a snapshot of Mrs. Kennedy. The sight of them sickened me.

I entered through the side door that led into a hallway adjacent to the kitchen. Provi happened to be in there, and when she saw me, tears filled her eyes.

"Hello, Mr. Hill," she said.

"Good morning, Provi," I answered. "How is she?"

"She slept some last night. And she's dressed."

"Let her know I'm here, will you?"

"*Sí, sí.* Madame wants to see you. Come, come." She motioned for me to follow her.

We walked through the dining and living rooms, then into the library in the back part of the house. Mrs. Kennedy was sitting at a desk, pen in her hand, writing away on one of her ever-present yellow legal pads.

She looked up when we walked into the room, and as our eyes met, she tried to force a smile. "Hello, Mr. Hill," she said. "It's nice to see you."

"It's nice to see you too, Mrs. Kennedy."

There was a pause as we looked at each other, then looked away. We were both struggling to hold it together.

"Have you talked with Nancy?" she asked. Nancy Tuckerman, one of Mrs. Kennedy's longtime friends, had replaced Tish Baldrige as her social secretary in May 1963.

"No, not yet. I came to see you first."

"I'm planning to go and thank the volunteers that Nancy organized to respond to all the mail. I'd like to thank them personally. She said Friday would be a good day. Can you work out the details with her?"

"Of course. Is there anything else you need?"

She looked at me, her eyes so filled with grief and emptiness. "Would you speak to Mr. Foster and tell him to make sure the agents take John outside each day? Just to the park or for a walk with his little tricycle so he gets some fresh air."

As soon as she mentioned John, a lump gathered in my throat. I had to get out of there.

"Of course," I said. "And I'll go call Nancy now."

The White House had received hundreds of thousands of letters and cards containing messages of sympathy for Mrs. Kennedy. While Mrs. Kennedy couldn't possibly answer every letter personally, she insisted that each one be acknowledged.

Nancy Tuckerman had organized teams of volunteers operating out of an office in the Executive Office Building next to the White House, and they'd been working tirelessly for weeks. Every piece of mail was opened, read, cataloged, and sent a response—an ivory card edged in black and crested with the Kennedy family coat of arms, preprinted with the message:

*Mrs. Kennedy is deeply appreciative of
your sympathy and grateful
for your thoughtfulness*

Congress had authorized Mrs. Kennedy franking privileges for the rest of her life, so in the upper right corner where a stamp would normally go, the envelopes were preprinted with her signature.

On Friday, January 10, Paul Landis and I took her to visit the volunteers. The staff had lined up to greet her, and as soon as she saw the familiar faces, she broke into a smile. When she walked into the office and saw the mountains of mail, she could hardly believe it. There were big canvas drawstring bags labeled U.S. MAIL piled up in one corner of the room and countless stacks of envelopes, all sizes and colors, in bins and boxes.

Mrs. Kennedy walked around and personally thanked each person. "Thank you so much for all you're doing," she said. "I think it's so important that each one of these letters be acknowledged, and I truly appreciate all of your efforts to make that happen."

Nancy handed her one of the letters that had just been opened and said, "We're setting aside the most interesting and poignant ones, so you can have them to read in your own time."

Mrs. Kennedy held the letter in her hands, and as she read it to herself, tears welled in her eyes. She looked up at Nancy and said, "The children and I loved Jack so much, but all these letters remind me that people all over the world loved him too. We're all heartbroken and wondering how we'll manage to go on."

She stayed just long enough to make sure the volunteers understood how grateful she was, and then we left. It was one of those crisp January days in Washington with not a cloud in the sky, and as we stepped outside, Mrs. Kennedy said, "Mr. Hill, it's such a beautiful day, why don't we take a walk through Lafayette Square."

Located directly across from the White House on Pennsylvania Avenue, Lafayette Square consists of a park filled with walking paths and surrounded by rows of nineteenth-century town houses. When President Kennedy came into office, there was a plan to raze many of the historic buildings and replace them with modern high-rise office buildings. Mrs. Kennedy convinced her husband that the new office buildings should be designed to preserve the charm and character of the existing structures. She lobbied Bernard Boutin, the General Services administrator, who made the final decisions, and I remembered her walking around the park with him pointing out all the architectural details she admired.

"In France there is a law providing that certain buildings of historical or architectural importance cannot be destroyed," she said. "It would be nice for Congress to have such a law here."

Mrs. Kennedy was instrumental in saving Lafayette Park, across the street from the White House. Here architect John Carl Warnecke (left) and GSA administrator Bernard Boutin (pointing) show Mrs. Kennedy a scale model of the new design in September 1962. Both she and her husband were proponents of saving buildings and landmarks with historical significance.

Top: Mrs. Kennedy graciously shakes hands with well-wishers as she walks through Lafayette Park, January 10, 1964.

Bottom: After visiting the volunteers who were painstakingly answering the condolence letters to Mrs. Kennedy, we walked through Lafayette Park. A photographer manages to catch Mrs. Kennedy, Paul Landis, and me in a rare moment of levity.

The architect John Carl Warnecke was hired to design a new plan and, sure enough, the GSA approved it. Mrs. Kennedy had saved Lafayette Park. And ultimately, in 1966, Congress passed the National Historic Preservation Act, which set federal policy for the preservation of our heritage and established both the National Register of Historic Places and the National Historic Landmarks Program, for which Jacqueline Kennedy deserves much credit.

While we had been inside with the volunteers, word had spread that Mrs. Kennedy was in the area, and people had gathered outside, hoping to see her.

"Hello, Mrs. Kennedy!" a woman called out. "It's so nice to see you out and about."

"Hello," she answered with a smile. It was the first time she'd been out in public since the assassination, and I was concerned about how she would handle this sudden unexpected attention.

"May I shake your hand, Mrs. Kennedy?" a woman asked. I moved closer to her, prepared to push the people away, but to my surprise, Mrs. Kennedy reached out her hand and said, "Of course."

She really seemed buoyed by the smiling people that had gathered to wish her well. As we rounded the corner to enter our car, a photographer walking backward, snapping away, smashed right into a garbage can. Paul Landis, Mrs. Kennedy, and I all burst into laughter. It actually turned out to be a pretty good photograph, and while it didn't make the papers, the photographer sent us each a copy.

Mrs. Kennedy was so moved by the massive outpouring of condolences that she decided she wanted to give a televised message to the nation. Four days later, with the president's brothers Bobby and Teddy seated across from her for moral support, she recorded a heartfelt message that was broadcast on television that evening to the American people. Looking straight into the camera, her voice low, calm, and steady, she said, "I want to take this opportunity to express my appreciation for the hundreds of thousands of messages—nearly eight hundred thousand in all—which my children and I have received over the past few weeks. The knowledge of the affection in which my husband was held by all of you has sustained me."

The slightest glint of tears began to well in her eyes when she admitted, "Whenever I can bear to, I read them."

She said that it was her wish for each letter to be acknowledged, but noted that it would take a long time to do so.

Speaking for less than two minutes, she concluded with a final thank-you on behalf of her children and the president's family "for the comfort your letters have brought to us all."

She showed remarkable grace and strength. I was proud of her.

In those first few months of 1964, we were constantly on the go. I don't think I realized it at the time, but to be moving from one place to another, having trips on the horizon to both new places and those that were comfortable, was the only way Mrs. Kennedy was coping. She couldn't just stay in Washington, where there were reminders everywhere of what had been and what was lost. From Georgetown, you'd hear the unmistakable sound of the presidential helicopter overhead and your mind would go back to those glorious weekends at Wexford, where the president and Mrs. Kennedy had felt so relaxed, taking walks, riding horses, entertaining friends. So full of hope for the future.

The sound of the helicopter was just one reminder of the privileges we no longer had available. As soon as Mrs. Kennedy moved out of the White House on December 6, instead of driving her around in the elegant limousine that was part of the White House presidential fleet, we used a station wagon. I couldn't call for a police escort to clear the roads when we went to the airport; I couldn't just call the White House operator to connect me to anyone in the world; I didn't have a secretary to type up itineraries or keep track of expenses. I had a little green memorandum book I always carried in my suit-jacket pocket, in which I kept important phone numbers, like those of the Kennedy family members, and jotted down flight numbers, arrival and departure times, and any other necessary logistical details. I was compelled to do everything in my power to ease the burdens for Mrs. Kennedy. Researching the most efficient way to get from one place to another, whether by plane, boat, or car; planning and thinking of everything that could go wrong and how to avoid it so that she didn't have to worry.

Meanwhile, the nation was obsessed with the assassination and trying to determine if Lee Harvey Oswald had indeed been the assassin and if he had acted alone. You couldn't turn on the radio or the television or look at a newspaper without some mention of it. Mrs. Kennedy's constant activity kept my mind focused, so that my thoughts didn't have a chance to wander back to Dallas.

On January 19, Mrs. Kennedy attended a memorial Mass at the Cathedral of the Holy Cross in Boston. The Solemn Pontifical Mass of Requiem was by invitation only—for 1,800 guests—but was being broadcast live on television throughout the country. Meanwhile, thousands more had jammed the streets

Walking with Mrs. Kennedy and Richard Cardinal Cushing as they enter the Cathedral of the Holy Cross in Boston for the Requiem Mass, January 19, 1964.

Mrs. Kennedy wipes a tear as she sits next to her brother-in-law Ted and mother-in-law, Rose, at the Requiem Mass in Boston, January 19, 1964. The poignant music from the Boston Symphony Orchestra and a 180-person choir was soul-stirring.

around the historic Gothic cathedral, hoping to see Mrs. Kennedy and to pay their respects. Mrs. Kennedy held on to her brother-in-law Senator Ted Kennedy as she walked up the steps to the grand front entrance, where Richard Cardinal Cushing, the archbishop of Boston and longtime close friend and spiritual advisor to the Kennedy family, waited to greet them. I walked behind, trying to give them space, but keenly aware that this large gathering was the kind of thing that made Mrs. Kennedy uncomfortable. She knew everyone was watching her, the photographers waiting for her to shed tears so they could catch her grief in a snapshot to splash onto the front page of every newspaper across the country. She was so fragile, and she seemed to be getting thinner all the time. I worried she might faint.

The ceremony was extremely moving, something everyone in attendance would never forget. Seated in the front pew next to her mother-in-law, Rose, her brother-in-law Teddy, and his wife, Joan, Mrs. Kennedy brushed away tears at times, as Mozart's Requiem in D Minor was performed with magnificent perfection by the Boston Symphony Orchestra and a 180-voice choir. It was an emotional experience to be surrounded by hundreds of people sitting respectfully in silence and praying for the slain president, as the solemn music echoed throughout the vast chamber with the sopranos reaching notes so angelic, you couldn't help but feel it deep into your soul. I never experienced anything like it before or since.

Mrs. Kennedy had learned that the house across the street from the Harrimans' house was coming up for sale, and after touring it, she decided it would be ideal for her and the children. The historic brick colonial at 3017 N Street NW had numerous bedrooms and bathrooms, large areas for entertaining, and a private backyard. It was on a quiet street but within walking distance to Georgetown shops and restaurants and the Chesapeake & Ohio Canal Towpath.

When she told me she had purchased the house, I expressed my congratulations and added, "It's a great location, Mrs. Kennedy. Very close to the path along the canal."

"Remember when we'd walk up and down that path when I was out to here with John?" She held her hand out in front of her flat stomach, exaggerating how big she was when she was pregnant.

"I do indeed," I said. It seemed a lifetime ago. "The first time we met, I remember you telling me you didn't want the agents following you around like puppy dogs."

"And I still don't," she said with a smile. "But I understand now that everything you do, you do for my own well-being and for the safety of the children." Tears began to well in her eyes and I had to look away. "Oh, Mr. Hill," she added, "I hope you know how much I appreciate you."

"I do, Mrs. Kennedy. I do."

I thought back to the day after the election in 1960, when I was first told by the chief of the Secret Service, U. E. Baughman, that I was being assigned to Mrs. Kennedy. I had been on the detail protecting President Dwight D. Eisenhower for the previous year, had traveled all over the world, and was proud to be part of that elite group of men. So when Chief Baughman told me I was being moved to the protection of the first lady, it was like a punch in the gut. I was devastated. It was like being moved from the starting lineup to the bench. I had visions of standing around at tea parties and canasta games because that's what the agents who had been assigned to Mamie Eisenhower and Bess Truman did.

As it turned out, I had the best job in all of the Secret Service. It was much different and far more rewarding than I had anticipated. Mrs. Kennedy was extremely spontaneous, so I had to be on my toes at all times. We were always on the go. I dealt with her directly rather than through a supervisor, so it was more of a one-on-one situation, which made the job much more personal. But that also meant a great deal more responsibility than working on a shift with a group of other agents.

After Agent Jeffries was reassigned during our trip to India and Pakistan, I was the sole agent on her detail for the next several months. One Secret Service agent protecting the first lady of the United States. I slept when she slept. And when she was awake, I was on duty. I was there to take her wherever she wanted to go. Often it was just the two of us in the car, or just us and a driver. We would talk about upcoming plans, or issues with the children, or whatever was on her mind. I was a good listener, and she knew that whatever was said in the car would not go any further.

My priority, always, was her protection. But because we spent so much time alone together and genuinely enjoyed each other's company, the lines blurred at times between what was personal and what was professional. It was my job to protect her, but I also cared about her. I didn't have to say it. She knew it.

What also went unsaid was what we both knew lay ahead. The time would come when I would leave. When she no longer qualified for Secret Service protection.

She had given me a copy of a long letter she'd written shortly after the assassination to Treasury Secretary Douglas Dillon. The letter was flowing with gratitude and compliments about all of the agents assigned to her and the children—how devoted, clever, kind, and adaptable we were, and how our presence had made it possible for her family to have "the close happy life" they had. But the main purpose of the four-page letter was to request that each of us, when it was time to move on, be given special consideration to advance in the Secret Service—that is, to be moved into the more challenging and esteemed positions on the President's Detail or other supervisory roles, rather than be "left in the backwater" of protecting a former first lady and her children.

I was thirty-two years old. I had my whole career in the Secret Service ahead of me. And while neither of us could speak about it yet, my inevitable departure hovered over us like a dark cloud.

S he never asked my opinion about security issues at the new house or expressed any concern about where the agents would be posted. By this time,
she knew that I would figure out how best to ensure that she and the children
were safe, wherever she chose to live.

She enlisted the help of Billy Baldwin, one of her decorator friends, to make
the interior suitable and to her taste, and for a while, it seemed, this gave her
something on which to focus her attention.

February 4, 1964,
was moving day.
Mrs. Kennedy
hand-carries a
stack of books
into her newly
purchased
residence in
Georgetown,
assisted by Robert
Kennedy Jr. and
Brumus, the dog.
She hoped she
could settle in
with her children
and live a private,
normal life.

Top: Some of the ever-present tourists, standing on the opposite side of the street taking photos of Mrs. Kennedy's new home, hoping to catch her coming out the door and down the steps.

Bottom: Every time we left the house, there were people staked out across the street taking photos. We tried to do everything we could to cut down on the tourists, and police had cordoned off a portion of the street, but nothing worked. Here Mrs. Kennedy and Lee keep their heads down, while I walk behind them with decorator Billy Baldwin, glaring at the tourists.

February 4, 1964, was moving day. It was a short distance across the street, but most things were coming by van from storage, having been placed there upon Mrs. Kennedy's departure from the White House two months earlier. Attorney General Robert Kennedy showed up to assist, along with one of his sons and their big slobbering Newfoundland, Brumus. Bobby took that damn dog practically everywhere he went.

The street was blocked off to traffic and we had some police officers posted outside, but hundreds of people, mostly women, lined the sidewalk across the street watching Mrs. Kennedy walk back and forth from the Harrimans' to her new residence carrying box after box of books and papers. Those prying eyes made all of us feel very uncomfortable, but there wasn't much we could do. It was a public street, and Mrs. Kennedy was now an ordinary citizen. I think she thought she could just meld back into some semblance of a private life, while I too thought that, over time, people would lose interest in her now that she was no longer the first lady. Boy, was I wrong.

18

STOWE & ANTIGUA

MARCH/APRIL 1964

T he Kennedys always spent Easter in Palm Beach, so I was quite surprised when Mrs. Kennedy told me they were doing something different this year.

"Have you ever gone downhill skiing, Mr. Hill?"

"I'm afraid not. Didn't have that kind of landscape in North Dakota."

"I never have either. Bobby says I'll love it. He has convinced me to take the children skiing in Vermont over Easter."

"Whatever you want to do, Mrs. Kennedy, is what we are going to do."

"Bobby says it's much better for the children to learn while they're young." She seemed to be trying to convince herself that this was a good idea. "Teddy will be there, and Eunice and Sarge . . . And of course it will be good for John and Caroline to be with all their cousins."

"Of course," I echoed. "It sounds like a lot of fun. Just give me as many details as possible ahead of time."

We didn't have email or texting in those days, but we communicated in a similar way—with notes back and forth—and I would often try to add a bit of humor.

MARCH 19, 1964

MRS. KENNEDY

Nancy T. called. Pam is out of town so she is handling clothes right now.

You had seen some sketches in the *New York Times*, one of which was a pair of Evening Pajamas. They are $110.00 and come from Ohrbach's. There are no charge accounts at Ohrbach's so Nancy needs to know if it would be o.k. to use your name in purchasing the p.j.'s so that they can be returned in the event you do not like them—or what should she do? Also what size, 10 or 12?

Sincerely
Ives St. Laurent Hill

The note came back to me with Mrs. Kennedy's handwritten reply: "Size 10—Couldn't she put them in Ethel or Joan's name—If not—I guess mine is ok."

For the next few days, she called me Monsieur St. Laurent, and sometimes it came with a little smile.

The notes were going back and forth as Mrs. Kennedy tried to organize the proper attire for her ski holiday.

"Oh, Mr. Hill, will you please get this to Nancy?" she asked as she handed me a cryptic handwritten note. "She'll understand what it all means."

As I tried to decipher her notations about various sizes of boots being too tight around the ankle, she said, "Bobby says it's terribly important I have comfortable ski boots. But I can't imagine how any of them will be comfortable at all."

All the arrangements were being made for the ski trip to Stowe, Vermont, when Mrs. Kennedy threw me a curve.

"I know how you hate last-minute changes, Mr. Hill," she said, "but I've decided to cut the ski trip short and go somewhere warm with Lee and Stash. Please send this telegram to Marietta Tree right away. I'll let you know as soon as we have everything firmed up."

She gave me a telegram addressed to Mrs. Ronald Tree in Saint James, Barbados, kindly requesting if she could use their house the first week of April. She apologized for the terribly short notice and hoped it wouldn't create any difficulties.

Mrs. Kennedy with Caroline and John on their first ski trip. Stowe, Vermont, March 1964.

As it turned out, Mr. and Mrs. Tree were using their house in Barbados and had a houseful of guests. After a few more telegrams, Mrs. Kennedy had secured the home of Bunny and Paul Mellon in Antigua. Of course, I knew the plans could still change, but I went to work organizing flights and other logistics. As long as I was busy, I didn't have time to think. And I was sure Mrs. Kennedy was feeling the same way. As long as we had a trip to plan, somewhere new to go, lots of activities, you could put one foot in front of the other.

The Kennedys had booked a wing of rooms at a lodge at the base of Mount Mansfield. Bobby and his family had been there before, so he had taken care of the arrangements and had organized ski instructors for Mrs. Kennedy, Caroline, and John.

Caroline and John took to the sport easily, while Mrs. Kennedy slowly got the hang of it, starting on the bunny slope with the children. As long as there was activity, Mrs. Kennedy was fine. The evenings were the most difficult, when everyone retired to their separate rooms.

Mrs. Kennedy and Caroline attended Easter Mass on Sunday, then followed everyone else onto the slopes. Easter had always been spent in Palm Beach with President Kennedy's father and mother. But, like Christmas, it was never going to be the same again. New memories, new traditions had to be made.

Mrs. Kennedy left John and Caroline in the care of Ethel Kennedy, the nannies, and Agents Tom Wells, Lynn Meredith, and Bob Foster in Stowe and flew with Bobby to New York City. Lee and Stash met us in New York, and we all flew commercial down to Antigua.

The Mellon property was a private oasis overlooking the turquoise water of Half Moon Bay. Wandering paths led through gardens of brilliant tropical plants to the main house and swimming pool, a greenhouse, and small pink guesthouses. Everywhere you looked, you could see the shimmering water that seemed to go on forever. It was beautiful, private, and very quiet.

Mrs. Mellon had warned Mrs. Kennedy that she had two decorative painters there—Bill and Paul—who were staying in one of the guesthouses. Paul Landis and I could stay in one of the others.

Paul and I had been working with Mrs. Kennedy together now for a year and a half. We got along well and were as close as brothers. We'd always kidded around with each other and played harmless practical jokes, but ever since the assassination the levity was gone. We would look into each other's eyes and see the hollowness that time wasn't healing.

In Dallas, I was on the left side of the follow-up car in the forward position and Paul was in the rear position on the right side. We had both witnessed the horror before our eyes. There was no doubt that we were both suffering the same guilt, the same feelings of failure. And yet, neither of us could bear to speak about it. We never discussed that tragic day, nor the soul-crushing days that followed. Marching next to Mrs. Kennedy and the dead president's two brothers from the White House to St. Matthew's Cathedral; standing near her as she lit the Eternal Flame; desperately trying to remain stoic as Air Force One flew overhead and dipped its wings.

Now here we were in Antigua, in a place most people would consider paradise. And yet no amount of wealth or beauty or hospitality could fill the emptiness in our hearts.

Mrs. Kennedy was religious about writing thank-you notes and ordered personalized stationery by the case. She was anxious to show her gratitude to Mrs. Mellon for loaning the house on such short notice and, soon after we arrived, she asked me to send a telegram to her friend in Upperville, Virginia.

Mrs. Kennedy
helps John as
the ski instructor
looks on.

She addressed it "Dearest Bunny" and thanked her profusely for her generosity. She described the home and its grounds as "paradise," which inspired her to paint birds and flowers, while Stash wanted to paint floors with the two decorators, Bill and Paul. Meanwhile, she wrote, Bobby had discovered "a mountain of books" that he was devouring.

She signed it "Mrs. Smith."

The "Mrs. Smith" was her trying to add a dash of subtle humor—like me signing my name Ives St. Laurent Hill—and while it was true the place was beautiful and Bobby frequently had his head down in a book, the reality was that everyone was desolate.

They would go swimming in the clear Caribbean water, and a couple of afternoons they went waterskiing, but the activity wasn't enough to boost anyone's spirits. There was this overwhelming sense of despair, and you could just see it on their faces and in every facet of their bodies. I think Mrs. Kennedy had hoped this getaway outside the country would help all of them to move forward—like the trip on the *Christina* did for her after the death of Patrick—but being on that quiet island only seemed to emphasize the emptiness.

At the end of April, we went to New York for the World's Fair. She wanted to take the children and remain unobtrusive, but it was impossible. People started recognizing them, word got around, and we ended up cutting the visit short.

On May 26 we were back to New York for a press preview of the John F. Kennedy Presidential Library Exhibit, a collection of Kennedy memorabilia that was opening at the IBM Building, at Madison Avenue and 57th Street. The exhibit was going to travel around the country, visiting twenty-three cities to raise money for the Kennedy Library to be built in Boston.

It was her first formal appearance since the funeral, and I was concerned about her.

As she moved among the familiar objects, each with a thousand bittersweet memories attached—the president's desk and rocking chair, a book of poetry, an ancient statue he bought for himself in Rome, a pair of carved birds that Mrs. Kennedy had given him—Mrs. Kennedy commented, "Some people did not know how much he loved old and beautiful things, but it was just that beauty and grace that often moved him most."

She stopped in front of a series of family photographs that showed the late president campaigning, sailing the *Victura*, playing with John and Caroline.

"I suppose the photographs are the hardest to look at," Mrs. Kennedy said, her voice so somber amid the mementos of happier days.

Here is a typical
reaction when
a photographer
would call out,
"Mrs. Kennedy,
look over here!"
Mrs. Kennedy had
long since learned
to ignore them, but
a passerby would
do a double take.
At the World's Fair
in New York, the
unwanted attention
became too much
and we had to
leave.

Mrs. Kennedy clutches Caroline's hand as they walk into St. Matthew's Cathedral in Washington to attend Mass on what would have been John F. Kennedy's forty-seventh birthday. Photographers are lined up outside to capture her grief. The fascination with her and the children was relentless.

Friday, May 29. The president's birthday. That morning, I accompanied Mrs. Kennedy and Caroline to Mass at St. Matthew's Cathedral in Washington. Photographers had lined up outside, and as Mrs. Kennedy clutched her daughter's hand, trying to avoid the flashes, I couldn't help but feel a sense of sorrow and helplessness. All she wanted was privacy. Later, we went to Arlington Cemetery. John and Caroline were dressed in matching ivory coats, while she was still in mourning black. As she and the children knelt at the grave, the Eternal Flame dancing with life, I stood stoic as a corpse. The crowds were held back by rope lines, but they were watching her every move. She couldn't even visit her deceased husband in private.

Top: May 29, 1964: I'm walking behind, at right, as Mrs. Kennedy guides John and Caroline toward the gravesite of their father.

Bottom: I watch (behind the fence, at left), as Mrs. Kennedy and the children kneel and pray in front of the Eternal Flame. Standing directly behind her are Pat Kennedy Lawford, and Bobby and Ethel Kennedy with six of their children.

A year earlier, I'd been aboard the presidential yacht USS *Sequoia* for President Kennedy's forty-sixth birthday. And while I had no false illusions about my position—I was there to do a job, not as an invited guest—it was one of those extraordinary evenings that made me pause and realize what a rare and privileged life I was living. Not once had I ever imagined how it could all come crashing down.

Many of the birthday presents for President Kennedy were gag gifts. Seen in this photo are Sargent Shriver, Teddy Kennedy, President Kennedy, Mrs. Kennedy (standing), Eunice Kennedy, and Senator George Smathers. David Niven and Lem Billings are seated in front.

At his forty-sixth birthday party aboard the
USS *Sequoia*, President Kennedy (standing)
thanks everyone in attendance in a joking way.
He had a wonderful sense of humor.

Between April and June in 1964, the crowds of gawkers lining the sidewalks in front of her Georgetown house became worse and worse. Each morning busloads of tourists would show up, cameras at the ready, hoping they'd be lucky enough to catch Mrs. Kennedy coming or going. The way the house was situated, there was no way to get to the car except out the front door and down the steps to N Street.

"Mr. Hill," she'd plead, "can't you do something to make them stop?"

"I know it's terrible, Mrs. Kennedy. We've been discouraging people from gathering in proximity to your new home, but they continue to do so anyway. We have also talked with the owner of the tour bus company that has started using your home as a point of interest, but he has refused to cooperate. Apparently, he has the right to operate his buses on a city street, which N Street is. The only thing we've been able to do successfully is place officers on the sidewalk to tell people to keep moving."

I knew how much she craved privacy, but now the problem was that, because she was no longer first lady, we didn't have the influence we did at the White House. She knew it too, and this was just one more reminder of how her life would never be the same.

"I'm sorry, Mrs. Kennedy. But that is all we can legally do. I've asked our legal department to assist and help us come up with any alternative solutions."

It got so that she wanted to be anywhere but in her new home. We were back and forth to Wexford, where she'd ride Sardar, but even riding and being with her horse-loving friends didn't bring her joy like it always had.

The one place she seemed to feel most comfortable—and this didn't surprise me—was New York City.

It always felt so empty coming back to Washington. There was a new house, but there were always gawkers, and everywhere you went there were reminders of President Kennedy. His absence was so present there.

19

———

NEW YORK CITY

———

1964

ew York City was the one major metropolitan city Mrs. Kennedy had visited regularly while she was first lady. She would fly in and stay at the Carlyle Hotel, at 76th and Madison, which became our operational base. The location was ideal for many reasons. It was relatively quiet, as far as New York City is concerned, and was one block from the apartment of President Kennedy's youngest sister, Jean, and her husband, Steve Smith, at 950 Fifth Avenue. It was one block from Central Park and not far from the Metropolitan Museum of Art. The Kennedys had a leased apartment that took up the thirty-fourth and thirty-fifth floors of the hotel, but after the president was assassinated, Mrs. Kennedy requested a smaller suite—one that still had a grand view of Central Park and plenty of space, but without the jolting memories.

Mrs. Kennedy had always felt comfortable in New York, and the Carlyle Hotel was like a second home to her. She had come to realize that, inevitably, there would be photographers waiting outside the iconic revolving doors. She would emerge with a smile, so they could get one good photograph and then, hopefully, leave her alone.

While it might seem surprising, New York City actually provided something of an escape from the paparazzi and general gawking public. There were fewer tourists in those days, and the local New Yorkers always seemed to be in such a rush to get from Point A to Point B that they paid very little attention to who or what they walked by. The hustle and bustle of the city turned out to be advantageous to Mrs. Kennedy, and to me as well.

She had some regular places she frequented. Her hairdresser, Mr. Kenneth, at 19 East 54th, for example. Bonwit Teller. Dining at the Four Seasons, Lutèce, Le Pavillon, River Club, and Giovanni's. She would lunch with Kitty Carlisle Hart, who always had the best New York gossip, and her sister-in-law Jean Kennedy Smith, but otherwise she had few female friends. Besides Bobby, she turned to other men whose opinions she valued for counsel and guidance: André Meyer, a French American investment banker and advisor to the Kennedys, who also lived at the Carlyle; Chuck Spalding, a longtime friend and former classmate of President Kennedy's; Irwin Shaw, an American playwright and novelist; and Steve Smith, Jean's husband. These were people who were giving her advice, and she was picking their brains as best she could.

She might go to a party hosted by Vincent Price at his apartment or travel out to the country estate of Truman Capote with Lee, who was a close friend of Capote's. Before the assassination she was a frequent attendee at Broadway plays. Now, in 1964, she shied away from such public outings. Staying busy, moving about and always on the go, seemed to be her way of dealing with the emotional trauma we all carried with us. That constant activity was also what kept me sane.

After one trip to New York, we were driving back to her house in Georgetown from the airport. As was usual, an agent from the local field office was driving, I was in the right front seat, and Mrs. Kennedy was in the back.

"Mr. Hill," she said.

"Yes, Mrs. Kennedy?" I answered, turning around to face her.

"You know," she said, "I told everyone—and I really believed it—that I'd go on living in the places I lived with Jack: in Georgetown and at the Cape. But every time I come back here, after being away, whether it's New York or our little trips to Vermont and Antigua, it's so empty and depressing."

I nodded. I knew exactly how she felt.

The doormen at the Carlyle were the best. They never revealed if she was staying there or not, and they watched out for her as if they were honorary Secret Service agents.

"Those three years in the White House were really the happiest, and now they're all gone." The longing in her voice was crushing. But I felt it too. There was a pall of sadness whenever we were in a place where we'd been with the president.

"What do you think about me moving to New York?" she asked. "I mean, permanently." I had anticipated this was coming and had indeed thought about it.

"Mrs. Kennedy, even though New York City is larger and much more densely populated than D.C., I have noticed a different attitude there. New Yorkers, and even the tourists, seem to be so preoccupied with themselves and their surroundings that they ignore people walking by them. That is all to your advantage. New York may very well be much better than D.C. for you and the children."

While Mrs. Kennedy was trying to decide whether to move to New York, unbeknownst to me, Paul Landis was mulling his own future. The morning of June 12, Paul reported for duty and handed in his resignation. I was stunned. But at the same time, I understood. We were the only two agents assigned to Mrs. Kennedy. And while our colleagues on the President's Detail worked in shifts and had regular days off, Paul and I had no one to replace us. Day after day, seven days a week—it didn't matter if we were in Washington or Hyannis Port or Antigua—just being around Mrs. Kennedy and the children was a constant reminder of the tragedy we had failed to prevent. It had become too painful.

Now, once again, I was solely responsible for Mrs. Kennedy's protection.

The next time we went back to New York, Mrs. Kennedy began house hunting in earnest, with the help of André Meyer, who was instrumental in helping her locate a suitable property that was within her means.

It was on June 29 that she first visited 1040 Fifth Avenue. We flew in from Hyannis Port that morning. I took her to Mr. Kenneth to get her hair done, and then Mr. Meyer met us at 1040. I stood outside the entryway as they toured the spacious duplex apartment on the fifteenth floor. She loved the light and the large windows that looked out over Central Park. And it was conveniently located, just a few blocks from her brother- and sister-in-law, Steve and Jean Smith.

"Of course, it will need to be completely redecorated," she said. "But look at the marvelous view!" We were there an hour and nine minutes. And then she and André Meyer went back to the Carlyle to discuss the financials.

The children mostly stayed in Hyannis Port that summer, but Mrs. Kennedy was restless. She was deeply involved in the planning and design of the John F. Kennedy Presi-

Lee, Mrs. Kennedy, me, and Stash Radziwill, walking in New York City. The photographers would walk backward to catch a photograph, calling out to Mrs. Kennedy to smile. She'd look away and I'd stare them down, imploring them with my eyes to just leave her alone. If I made a scene, it would be even worse. There was nothing we could do but walk fast and get inside.

dential Library, which would be built in Boston, so she was meeting with the world-renowned architectural firms Skidmore, Owings & Merrill in New York City and with Mies van der Rohe in Chicago. We were moving up and down the East Coast—sometimes flying, sometimes driving—between Hyannis Port, Washington, and New York. I barely had time to stop at home and get laundry and dry cleaning done before we were off again.

July 28 was her thirty-fifth birthday. She had never really made a big deal out of her birthday, but this was her first without her husband. We were in Hyannis Port and she had planned to go to Newport with the children, but at the last minute she told me we were flying to New York on the *Caroline*, the Kennedy family plane.

A press photographer was rarely able to get inside the lobby of the Carlyle Hotel, but a lucky one got this shot of Mrs. Kennedy and me in the elevator. Mrs. Kennedy smiles graciously for the intruding photographer, while I pretend to be an anonymous guest with a good tan.

It was just the two of us aboard, and once we got settled, I said, "Happy birthday, Mrs. Kennedy."

She looked at me and tried to form a smile. "Thank you, Mr. Hill. It's really just another day, isn't it?" Her eyes were still so empty. Everyone always says time will heal, but when? How long? It didn't seem possible we'd ever heal.

Mrs. Kennedy's brother-in-law Steve Smith had arranged a dinner that night at the Four Seasons with a small group of trustees of the presidential library. It was just Mrs. Kennedy; her brothers-in-law Bobby and Steve; McGeorge Bundy, the former national security advisor; and Eugene Black, former president of the World Bank. They had a table in a private corner, and few people paid attention to them.

Around ten o'clock, Steve Smith came over to the table where I was sitting and said, "As soon as we can get rid of Black and Bundy, we're taking her to a discotheque."

"A what?"

"It's a private dance club in the basement of the Gotham Hotel, at Fifth and 55th. I thought you'd want to know."

Steve was good that way, keeping me informed so I could make the appropriate arrangements. I radioed Agent Hal Thomas, the New York Field Office agent who was driving the limousine for us, to let him know we would be coming out soon.

When they were ready to go, I made sure the car was out front so I could get her in the back seat with Bobby and Steve as quickly as possible.

As we pulled up to the Gotham—what is now the Peninsula—I pulled out my memo book and jotted down the time and address: *10:38 pm Le Interdite. [sic] 2 W. 55th Street.*

Steve Smith got out and went to speak with the club manager to let him know of the special guests that were arriving. He came back a few minutes later and said, "We're all set. A secluded table in a corner."

I knew that Bobby, who was still the attorney general at that time, and Steve were doing their damnedest to try to raise Mrs. Kennedy's spirits, especially on this first birthday since her husband was killed. Mrs. Kennedy was more curious about this new phenomenon that had been imported from France than anything else. The disco was dark, with flashing lights, and people were dancing to the loud beat of recorded music. The three of them stayed huddled at their table, while I stood as inconspicuously as possible nearby. It was after one o'clock in the morning when we finally departed—leaving as briskly as we had arrived. No one ever realized that the current attorney general and the former first lady of the United States—the most famous woman in the world—were in their midst.

In the car on the way back to Steve Smith's residence, they were all laughing, going back over the night and the people they'd seen, amazed that no one had recognized them. I realized that was probably the best birthday gift she could have had: anonymity.

20

—

ONE LAST TRIP

—

AUGUST 1964

In early July Mrs. Kennedy informed me that she was considering a trip in August.

"Charles and Jayne Wrightsman have invited Lee and me to join them for a cruise down the Dalmatian coast and around the boot of Italy on a private yacht they've chartered. Departing Venice on August 6. We'll be gone a week or two."

Jayne and Charles Wrightsman were Palm Beach neighbors of President Kennedy's parents, and when Mrs. Kennedy was trying to raise money to restore the White House, the Wrightsmans donated $500,000 worth of antiques to the effort. While Mrs. Kennedy and Jayne shared an appreciation of fine art, their friendship had seemed to me more superficial, certainly not as close as her relationship with Eve Fout or Bunny Mellon.

I jotted down some notes as she told me the details. "I would like to fly to London, stay overnight with Stash and Lee. Lord and Lady Harlech are coming too, so we'll all fly together to Venice."

"Are you bringing the children?" I asked.

"Not this time. Caroline and John will be staying with my mother in Newport."

I was taken by surprise that she was willing to be away from the children for such a long period of time.

"Will you be sending anyone ahead in advance?" she asked.

"I would prefer to do that, but let me check into it," I said. With Paul Landis gone, I had to request additional assistance.

"You know, Mr. Hill, I've been thinking about something. It's been on my mind for a while. Would it be possible to give the assignment to one of the men who has been working with the children who never gets to travel on these foreign trips?"

"That's very thoughtful of you, Mrs. Kennedy. Let me see what I can arrange. I know a few men who would really appreciate that opportunity."

I went to the office and sat down to try and put all the pieces together. Of the three agents working with Caroline and John, Lynn Meredith and Bob Foster had both had some travel opportunities, but Tom Wells had not.

I didn't have much information about any fixed itinerary other than a departure date, but when I mentioned it to Wells, he said, "Count me in!"

My good friend Paul Rundle, who had been one of my early mentors when I joined the Secret Service in the Denver Field Office, was now handling our European operations from Paris. Rundle had been standing on the South Portico of the White House when we brought President Kennedy's body back from Bethesda Naval Hospital the morning of November 23.

"What can I do to help, Clint?" he had asked. "I'll do anything you need me to do." His being there and making that sincere offer meant a lot to me. I hadn't spoken to him since he'd taken the transfer to Paris, but when I called him about Mrs. Kennedy's trip, he was eager to help.

On August 5, 1964, Mrs. Kennedy and I boarded Pan Am Flight 100 in New York at the newly renamed John F. Kennedy International Airport and flew off to London.

Prince Radziwill and Agent Rundle were waiting at the airport in London when we arrived. Mrs. Kennedy practically jumped into Stash's arms when she saw him.

"Oh, Stash!" she exclaimed with delight. "You're a sight for sore eyes!"

Rundle reached out his hand to me with a smile. "Great to see you, Clint. The car is waiting."

Left: Mrs. Kennedy and Prince Stash Radziwill had a mutual admiration and love for each other. She was so surprised and happy to see him greet her at the airport in London. August 6, 1964.

Right: There was nothing romantic, but Stash and Mrs. Kennedy trusted, admired, and respected each other. I always had a great relationship with him too. He was just a genuine man. When he offered me a guest bedroom in his home in London, complete with his butler Stanley at my disposal, I didn't know what to say. It was his way of thanking me for everything I'd done.

When we arrived at the Radziwill residence at 4 Buckingham Place and I started pulling out Mrs. Kennedy's baggage, she and Prince Radziwill looked at each other like they had some big secret.

"Clint," Stash said, "don't touch that. You are my guest here. You'll be staying in the master guest suite and Stanley, my butler, will attend to your every need."

I was stunned. I had planned to stay in a nearby hotel.

"But . . . what?" I didn't know how to react or what to say. I was being treated as a guest of Prince and Princess Radziwill in their London home. I looked over at Mrs. Kennedy with a questioning look.

She just looked back at me with a broad smile on her face.

"Thank you, sir," I said. And off I went to my room with Stanley toting my luggage. Agent Rundle had the residence secured, so there really wasn't anything I had to do except relax. It was just for one night, but the gesture spoke volumes. Stash and Lee had accompanied Mrs. Kennedy on so many of her trips abroad, and they knew I always went out of my way to make sure everything went smoothly for them as well. We didn't necessarily have agents protecting them, but, invariably, Lee would ask me to do something to help her—whether it was getting a driver's license or her passport renewed—and I always obliged. I rationalized it by saying it wouldn't look good for Mrs. Kennedy if her sister got caught in some mess that the press would blow out of proportion. To be a guest in their home was the Radziwills' way of telling me they appreciated everything I had done for them over the years.

It was one of those things you never forget.

The next day we were off to Venice: Stash, Lee, Lord and Lady Harlech, Mrs. Kennedy, and me. The times I noted in my daily diary exemplify how much easier flight travel was in those days.

> *8:53 am JBK, Radziwills, Lord & Lady Harlech depart*
> *#4 Buckingham Place*
> *9:36 Arrive London Int'l VIP Lounge*
> *9:47 Depart VIP Lounge*
> *9:52 On Aircraft*
> *10:31 Depart via British European Airways*

There were no metal detectors, no taking off belts or shoes. I carried everyone's passports and boarding passes. Exactly sixteen minutes after our arrival at the airport, we were boarding the first-class compartment of the plane.

As I was helping Mrs. Kennedy get situated, Stash put his hand on my shoulder and said, "Clint, let the girls sit together, you sit next to me. We've got a lot of catching up to do."

I really liked Stash and I could tell he was trying to add some levity—trying to distract me from my thoughts, which, whenever there were idle moments, would take me back to Dallas. He succeeded in getting me to laugh a few times, and as we sat and talked, across the aisle from Mrs. Kennedy and Lee, on that short flight to Venice, he made me feel like I was his equal. Not a government employee there for a job, but like I was his friend. It was just a simple thing, but for a kid from North Dakota, to have a prince ask you to sit next to him was pretty special.

Agent Tom Wells was waiting for us in Venice, where he had done an outstanding job of making arrangements. We all boarded a motor launch and zipped out to the 188-foot luxury yacht *Radiant*. Mrs. Wrightsman took Mrs. Kennedy and the others on a tour of the boat, while I checked in with the captain and crew for a more thorough look around. It was important for me to see not only the areas the guests would use, but also the crew quarters, galley, laundry, and other working areas of the yacht. The *Radiant* wasn't as large or as lavish as the *Christina*, but no one was complaining.

We got underway, and forty minutes later the crew dropped anchor off the Lido di Venezia, a barrier island in the Venetian lagoon, for swimming and waterskiing. The water was warm and clear, and Mrs. Kennedy was beaming as the motor launch pulled her along the shore, with iconic Venice as the backdrop. Being on a yacht, far from the prying crowds, was really the best way for Mrs. Kennedy to travel and still maintain her privacy. Our itinerary was fluid, which made it difficult for the press to follow, and from the outset, it seemed like it was going to be an enjoyable trip. She seemed to be relaxed, and I thought that maybe this was just what she needed.

Dinner was served aboard the yacht at eight o'clock, and while the guests were eating, I went up to the bridge with the captain to observe as we weighed anchor. We cruised slowly along the coast for the next couple of hours, and then, at midnight, once everyone was tucked into their cabins, the captain turned and headed across the Adriatic Sea toward Yugoslavia. The second we entered Yugoslavian waters, we were escorted by a Yugoslavian naval security vessel, under the direct orders of Josip Broz Tito, president of Yugoslavia. It was shortly after eight in the morning when we arrived at the Zadar harbor. No sooner had we dropped anchor than Tom Wells radioed me with an unusual request.

"I'm on the Yugoslav vessel," he said. "And some of the navy officials want to pay their respects to Mrs. Kennedy. Is that all right?"

Mrs. Kennedy agreed, and for the next two hours she had coffee with the Yugoslavian officers, flattered by and appreciative of their condolences. Once they disembarked, we cruised to Starigrad, where we went ashore and toured an ancient castle. Even over here in Yugoslavia, Mrs. Kennedy was recognized by the locals as she walked along the stone balconies overlooking the Adriatic Sea. Everyone was very friendly, and she smiled graciously while shaking hands with the people she met.

The following morning, as we were cruising toward Dubrovnik, Mrs. Kennedy sent word that she wanted to talk to me. She was sitting on the deck with an empty chair next to her, where Mrs. Wrightsman had been.

"What can I do for you, Mrs. Kennedy?"

She motioned for me to lean in close to her. "Please go to the top deck near the smokestack," she whispered. "Make sure no one sees you, and I'll meet you there as soon as I can get away. I have something I need to discuss with you in private."

I had no idea what it could be, but I did as she asked and waited on the top deck. A short while later she appeared, and I could tell she was very anxious.

"What is it, Mrs. Kennedy? Are you ill?"

"Oh, Mr. Hill, I need you to get us off this boat," she said. "I just can't stay on here for the entire trip. I'll die of boredom."

I was really surprised. She had done a good job of pretending to be enjoying herself with Mrs. Wrightsman, but the mood on the *Radiant* certainly did feel a lot more staid and formal compared to the other yacht trips we had taken.

"Can you come up with an urgent reason for us to leave?" she pleaded.

"I will come up with something. But where do you want to go?"

"Lee and Stash have rented a villa in Porto Ercole," she said, looking around to make sure no one was near. "We can go there."

"Okay. I'll think of a viable excuse and get back to you as soon as possible."

Now I had to concoct a reason for all of us to leave the yacht, and it had to be something no one could question.

Lee and
Mrs. Kennedy
enjoy a tour
of the castle in
Hvar, Yugoslavia.
She loved the
architecture and
history there, but
she couldn't wait
to get off the
yacht with the
Wrightsmans.

It was nearly midnight when we pulled into Dubrovnik and docked at the pier, so you couldn't see much of anything. When the sun rose, I was impressed when I saw the massive walled city that towered in front of us. After breakfast, a guide took our group around the city for a quick one-hour tour. Mrs. Kennedy seemed to be genuinely interested. No one would ever guess she wasn't enjoying herself.

When we got back on board, we departed for Korčula. As soon as we were underway, I went to the bridge to speak to the captain.

"Captain," I said, "we got some intelligence that is very concerning. It's top secret, but I need to remove Mrs. Kennedy, her sister, and Stash from the yacht for security reasons. We have got to get to Naples as soon as possible. It's a matter of national security."

I was lying through my teeth, but it worked. I told Mrs. Kennedy my story and left it up to her to explain to her hosts the sudden change in plans.

Meanwhile, I contacted Tom Wells by radio and told him we were going straight to Naples from Korčula without stopping. When we disembarked, we would need ground transportation to take us to the nearest airport near our docking point at NATO headquarters, then an aircraft to take us from Naples to Fiumicino, outside of Rome, and ground transportation from there to the Villa Rossa in Porto Ercole. I knew that Wells had Henry Manfredi, a security officer at the U.S. Embassy in Rome, available to assist with anything we needed.

The next afternoon we arrived in Naples, where Mrs. Kennedy made her apologetic farewell to the very disappointed and concerned Wrightsmans. We promptly disembarked, drove to the airport, boarded a U.S. Embassy airplane, and flew to Fiumicino. We got into the cars waiting for us and drove from Fiumicino for almost three hours, arriving at the villa at about ten thirty that night. It had been a long day, but Wells and Manfredi had made it all work flawlessly.

When I go through TSA now, taking off my shoes, emptying my pockets into a bin, removing my belt, praying my pants don't fall down to my knees when I raise my hands above my head to walk through the metal detector, I sure miss those days. Traveling with Mrs. Kennedy was never predictable—it was always an adventure, and while it could be frustrating, it sure had its perks.

Mrs. Kennedy seemed much more carefree in Porto Ercole. She went to a beach every day and visited with the queen of the Netherlands and her husband, Prince Bernhard, who were summering in the nearby Villa L'Elefante Felice. She waterskied. She took a boat to a nearby island and spent time with Lee's children, Tony and Christina. She dined at the Prince Borghese villa and had dinner one night with Italian ambassador Egidio Ortona and his wife. The conversations were interesting, intelligent, and relaxed.

Even though our change of plans was kept very private, the paparazzi soon learned that Mrs. Kennedy was no longer on the *Radiant* and that she was now in Porto Ercole. She isn't pleased that the photographers got so close to her and her niece Christina, so I am moving in to intervene.

Waiting for a boat ride back to the villa. I always preferred to wear a blazer because I had pockets for everything. Sometimes it wasn't appropriate, like when you're on an island in Italy and everyone else is in bathing suits or casual clothes. I'd carry a TWA bag with me to hold everything. (I probably have everyone's shoes in there, as well as my own.) Porto Ercole, Italy, August 1964.

She could put on the charm when she needed to, and I'd seen her put on acts that could have won her an Academy Award. But once we got off the *Radiant*, I saw a change in her. She was beginning to enjoy life once again, but there was a determination about it. She was going to do it on her terms.

On August 20 she and I boarded TWA 841 at Fiumicino Airport to return to the United States. We arrived at JFK International, where a private Aero Commander was waiting, which flew us to the airport in Newport, Rhode Island. Caroline, John, and Mrs. Kennedy's mother and stepfather were there to meet us. It was wonderful to see Caroline, John, and their mother all squeezed together in one long embrace, just the way it should be. I breathed a sigh of relief, knowing we were back in the United States with one more adventure in my memory bank—this time a pleasant memory.

Passports and cigarette in one hand, I help Mrs. Kennedy figure out a couple of appropriate and meaningful gifts for John and Caroline at the airport in Rome before departing for the United States. This is one of my favorite photographs of the two of us. August 20, 1964.

21

MOVING ON

Upon my return from Italy, Chief James J. Rowley summoned me to his office. He asked me how everything was going with Mrs. Kennedy and the children, and we talked about her upcoming move to New York.

"Clint," he said, "we all know what a difficult year this has been, and you have handled it with your usual professionalism and dedication. After the election in November, we're reassigning you to the White House Detail."

It shouldn't have come as a surprise—the assignment to protect the former first lady had always been a temporary one—but still, to hear him say it with such finality gave me a pang of disappointment.

Rowley told me how highly valued I was to the Secret Service and that my leadership skills were needed for the presidential protective detail—whether that was going to be the incumbent, Lyndon Johnson, or the Republican nominee, Barry Goldwater.

"Yes, sir," I said.

Being on the President's Detail is where I had always wanted to be. I had thrived on the intensity of being with President Eisenhower, and the bond with the other agents was the closest thing to brotherhood I'd ever known. My wife and my two sons were in Virginia, and moving them to New York simply was not an option. These past several months—hell, these past four years—of constant travel had put a strain on my marriage. All the agents' wives complained—their husbands were always gone too. But none of them were with Jacqueline Kennedy. That was the difference.

I was with her.

It wasn't my choice to make. My job—and my allegiance—was to the U.S. Secret Service, not to an individual. It was time to move on.

As soon as I returned to her house, I asked if she had a few minutes, as there was something I needed to discuss with her.

"Of course, Mr. Hill," she said. "What is it?"

"Well, Mrs. Kennedy," I began, "I've just had a meeting with Chief Rowley, and he told me they want me to return to the White House after the election."

"Yes, I had a feeling," she said. "That's wonderful for you." She was trying to smile, but there was a wistfulness to her voice.

"I'll go with you to New York," I said. "Handle the move and anything else you need. And if there's anyone in particular you'd like assigned to your or the children's detail, just let me know."

"I know I'm being selfish when I say this," she said, "but it's hard to imagine what it will be like to not have you around."

"It's not selfish, Mrs. Kennedy," I answered. "I have mixed feelings about it myself."

She nodded and reached out to grab my hands. "The president and I talked about this often. How we hoped you and the other agents assigned to the children would be given opportunities to advance your careers. You deserve to move on. It's not fair for me to hold you back."

I gave her hands a squeeze as I saw tears welling in her eyes and felt the moisture in my own. I stepped back, and as we let go, both of us reached up to dab at our emotions.

"Thank you, Mrs. Kennedy. That means a lot to me."

The next day, Mrs. Kennedy requested to see me.

"I hope you don't mind, Mr. Hill, but I took the liberty to write a letter to Secretary Dillon after our conversation yesterday."

She handed me a mimeographed copy of a letter she had written.

"Go ahead and read it," she said. Then, with the glint of a sparkle in her eyes, she added, "I know you like to have as much information as possible."

The note was handwritten on her stationery, engraved MRS. JOHN F. KENNEDY at the top. Dated September 11, 1964. It was all about the Secret Service arrangements for herself and the children after she moved to New York on September 15. "I would like to ask that Clinton Hill—who will be assigned to another job—remain as overseer of our little detail," she began, noting that the new agents coming on board had not been with them at the White House. She realized I was going to be reassigned to another job in the near future but wanted to ensure that I would be able to remain with her as they settled into their new life in New York—staying the first couple of weeks at the Carlyle and then moving into the new apartment. She wrote that it would be "an enormous relief" if she knew that I could come back from time to time to solve or settle any problems and to accompany her on any foreign trips she might take, at least in the beginning.

She asked for some changes, noting that it really wasn't necessary for a Secret Service man to have to stand outside the building in the cold all night. She said she would abide by any decisions I made regarding security, but that her preference was to have enough protection for the children with as few agents as possible. For herself, she thought that her protection could be discontinued. She wanted to be able to walk around the city, take taxis, and do "all the little daily things" without two people constantly following. If she went to the theater or someplace there might be crowds, in those situations, she would want an agent with her.

As I read on, I started to get a lump in my throat as she described to Secretary Dillon how important I was to her.

"He is the only person who has known us for four years," she wrote, "whose judgment I trust and who I think is competent enough to set up the kind of detail I would like to have . . ."

She suggested we could put these theories to the test during the next month in New York and then I could devise a plan for the upcoming year.

I looked up at her and said, "Thank you for your kind words about me. I think this sounds like a good plan. We'll put it to the test and see how it goes."

The letter was her way of not quite letting me go.

And I didn't mind.

When we returned from Porto Ercole,
Mrs. Kennedy reluctantly agreed to let
Stanley Tretick do a photo shoot of her
and the children for *Look* magazine.
It was all for Bobby, to help him in his
campaign for the U.S. Senate.

*L*ook magazine was planning a memorial issue to be released around the first anniversary of the assassination, and while the rest of the Kennedy family had agreed to participate, Mrs. Kennedy wanted nothing to do with it. She was trying so desperately to move on with her life, but at the same time she was devoting herself to preserving her husband's memory. In the end, she reluctantly agreed to allow the photographer Stanley Tretick to come to Hyannis Port at the end of the summer to photograph her and the children for the special magazine issue. Bobby had announced he was running for the U.S. Senate representing New York, and she did it to help him more than anything.

Mrs. Kennedy and the children spent a few days in Newport at Hammersmith Farm with her mother and stepfather, and then on September 14 we all flew to New York. The apartment at 1040 Fifth Avenue was nearly ready, and now this new phase of Mrs. Kennedy's life was about to begin.

We checked into the Carlyle the day before Mrs. Kennedy and the children would be moving into their apartment. It had been arranged for me to stay in a small room at the

Carlyle for the next couple of months, until I returned to Washington. Before I met the Kennedys, I had never heard of anyone living in a hotel, and now here I was, living in not just any hotel but one of the finest in New York City.

As soon as I got Mrs. Kennedy situated in her suite, I asked, "What are your plans this afternoon, Mrs. Kennedy?"

It was a beautiful day, with not a cloud in the sky and just the slightest hint of crispness signaling that fall was on its way. Knowing her as I did, I figured she would want to have some kind of outdoor activity.

"Well, first I want to go over to 1040. And then, it's such a glorious day, we should take a walk in Central Park."

Suddenly, her eyes lit up and she added, "You know what I've always wanted to do?"

"I have no idea, Mrs. Kennedy," I said with a smile. "You never cease to surprise me."

"Oh, Mr. Hill!" She laughed. "I've always wanted to take the children out in one of those little rowboats on the lake in Central Park. Could you arrange that?"

"Of course," I said. "Whatever you want to do is what we're going to do."

Mrs. Kennedy's team of designers had furnished the apartment at 1040 Fifth Avenue to her specifications, and she was thrilled with the result. She took me on a tour, and as I looked around, I noticed that mementos from her various trips had been incorporated into the décor. There were things she'd purchased in Italy, gifts from Pakistan, a rosary from the pope. It was freshly painted, with new drapes and rugs, but the personal items made it feel like a home. Her home.

From there, we drove into Central Park, to the Loeb Boathouse, where I had arranged for an hour-long rowboat rental under the name of Hill.

No one paid any attention to the woman dressed in a suit and heels climbing into the rowboat with her young son and daughter. They were laughing and talking like any other mother and her children. I stood on the dock as Mrs. Kennedy handled the oars with ease, paddling the three of them around, weaving around the other boaters. At one point, I saw a young man rowing toward them, with a camera hanging around his neck. Suddenly he let go of the oars and put the camera up to his eyes to snap a photo of Mrs. Kennedy. He put the camera down, smiled, and waved, and she waved back. No harm done.

When we got back to the Carlyle, Mrs. Kennedy said, "See, Mr. Hill. I think everything's going to work out just fine."

In mid-September, Mrs. Kennedy and the children moved into their new apartment in New York City. It had a decorator's feel to it—refined and elegant—but she added her personal touch with many items she had collected on her travels around the world and the vast collection of books she and President Kennedy had accumulated.

When I picked up the newspaper the next morning, I was shocked to see the photo of Mrs. Kennedy and the children in the rowboat printed on an interior page. The photographer was apparently an amateur, but he was smart enough to know he could get paid for a candid photo like that and had sold it to the Associated Press.

September 14, 1964. "You know what I've always wanted to do?" she asked me. "I've always wanted to take the children out in one of those little rowboats on the lake in Central Park." She rowed around for a while in anonymity, but it wasn't long before someone in a nearby boat recognized her and took this photo.

Mrs. Kennedy wanted to walk Caroline and her niece Sydney home after Caroline's first day at her new school in New York. A crowd had started following her, and then a photographer ran ahead. Mrs. Kennedy instructed Caroline and Sydney to look straight ahead and not engage with the photographer or the growing crowd. "Just follow Mr. Hill," she said.

The next day was Caroline's first day at her new school. One of the reasons Mrs. Kennedy had found the apartment at 1040 so appealing was that it was a short five-and-a-half-block walk to the all-girls private Catholic school she had chosen for Caroline, the Convent of the Sacred Heart. Caroline was entering the second grade, and one of her cousins, Sydney Lawford, the daughter of President Kennedy's sister Pat and Peter Lawford, was also attending the school.

Caroline and Sydney were as excited as could be as they walked with their mothers that morning. They were greeted by some nuns and other classmates, and it looked like they were going to assimilate easily into the school.

Somehow word got out, and as Mrs. Kennedy walked home with the two girls later that day, a crowd started building around her. She held tightly to the girls' hands and said, "Don't look at anyone. Just keep your head down until we get home."

By the time she had returned to the apartment, she was visibly upset.

"Oh, Mr. Hill, what am I going to do? All I want is to be able to walk my daughter to school and back. Is that too much to ask?"

"I know, Mrs. Kennedy. I'd like to tell you that it's just the newness of you being in New York—and perhaps it is—but I think it's going to be this way for a while. I know how much you want to live your life without agents following you everywhere, but the truth is, the agents are going to allow you to do what you want to do. I'll make sure the new agents know that."

An office was set up for Mrs. Kennedy on Park Avenue, and Nancy Tuckerman had moved to New York to stay on as her assistant. I had started packing up my things at the Carlyle, getting ready to return to Washington.

The day before my departure, Mrs. Kennedy asked me to meet her in her office. When I walked in the door, I saw balloons and streamers.

"Surprise!"

There were just a few people there—Nancy, the small staff who worked with her, a handful of agents who worked with us from the New York Field Office, and of course, Mrs. Kennedy.

A large cardboard poster with a cutout picture of an anonymous Secret Service agent wearing sunglasses was standing on an easel. Above the agent, written in big letters, it said: MUDDY GAP WYOMING WELCOMES ITS NEWEST CITIZEN.

It was typical of Mrs. Kennedy's humor—an insinuation that I was being sent to some remote town out in the middle of nowhere.

We ate cake and everyone was reminiscing with funny stories. Then Mrs. Kennedy handed me a box.

She looked at me and said, in that soft, inimitable voice, "A little something, Mr. Hill. So you don't forget me."

I opened the box, and inside was a black three-ring binder. I flipped open the cover to reveal the first page:

It was a black piece of paper onto which had been pasted, in type: THE TRAVELS OF CLINTON J. HILL.

She had put together a scrapbook filled with photos from our various trips together. Greece, Morocco, India, Pakistan, Ravello. There were photographs inside that I'd never seen before. Page after page of Mrs. Kennedy and me together, and of her alone: swimming, waterskiing, posing in her bathing suit in Ravello, one in which she was in the water and had turned to look back at the camera, her hair mussed, her eyes twinkling with mischief.

But there were also pictures of me alone. One walking along the street in Ravello, barefoot, in my bathing suit. Another of Toby Chandler and me, taken from Gianni Agnelli's yacht, both of us in our bathing suits, sitting on the security boat, laughing.

I looked up at Mrs. Kennedy. "Where did you get these?"

She pursed her lips into a sly smile. "Oh, I have my ways, Mr. Hill."

On the last page was a photograph from our trip to Morocco. It was that wild night when we were carefree, laughing again after those difficult months following the death of baby Patrick. The last trip before everything changed.

In the photo we are walking with Moulay Abdallah, the king's brother. I am slightly behind her in a tuxedo, a cigarette in my hand. She is looking back at me and we are all laughing. On the photo she had written with a ballpoint pen:

Mr. Hill—Are you happy in your work?—JBK

She knew the answer to the question, of course. It was obvious.

I left for Washington the next day, and the following week, I was working on a shift protecting President Johnson at the LBJ Ranch in Texas.

I remained as a sort of informal supervisor over the Kennedy Protective Detail. She realized she and the children needed protection, and Congress ultimately approved agents for her until she remarried, and also for the children, each until they were sixteen.

She would call from time to time to ask my opinion about how things were being handled with the children's protection as they grew older. But I didn't see her again until June 1968, at Bobby's funeral. I had risen through the ranks and was, at that time, the Special Agent in Charge of presidential protection. I was there protecting President Lyndon Johnson.

We spoke briefly. Exchanged pleasantries. And that was the last time I ever saw her.

She married Aristotle Onassis later that year, and her Secret Service protection ended. I went on to serve two more presidents, ultimately becoming assistant director of the U.S. Secret Service, responsible for all protective activities.

Was I happy in my work? I've often said that being a Secret Service agent was the best job in the world. I'd still be working today if they'd let me.

22

———

FAREWELL

———

ALEXANDRIA, VIRGINIA, 2019

"Oh my God!" Lisa called out as she came running up the stairs from the basement. "I just found it. The scrapbook Mrs. Kennedy made for you. It was in the bottom of the trunk."

She had the binder in her hands and she put it on the dining-room table.

"That's it," I said.

Neither of us spoke as I slowly flipped through the pages. Each photograph brought back a rush of memories.

When I got to the last page, Lisa looked at me and said, "Some of these are really . . . intimate." She put her hand on my face and whispered, "Were you in love with her?"

The question took me by surprise. I had shared more with Lisa than I'd shared with anyone. I trusted her, implicitly, but still, I chose my words carefully.

"I wouldn't call it love. We had a bond, a bond that was really almost indescribable. I admired her and respected her. And I know she liked and respected me. We had fun times together and we shared the deepest tragedy. But it never could have been love. She was the wife of the president and I was there to protect her. And we both knew that. When I left New York, there was no other choice. It was time for both of us to move on with our lives."

Ever since I retired from the Secret Service in 1975, all people ever really wanted to talk to me about was that one day in Dallas. But as Lisa and I looked through the scrapbook together, I realized that was the one trip that was not included.

The photos Mrs. Kennedy had chosen and the humorous captions she had written brought back only good memories. I suppose that's what she'd hoped they would do.

THE TRAVELS OF CLINTON J. HILL

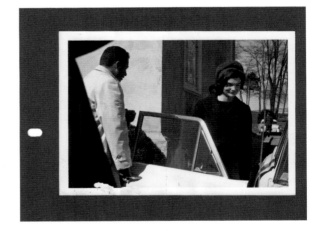

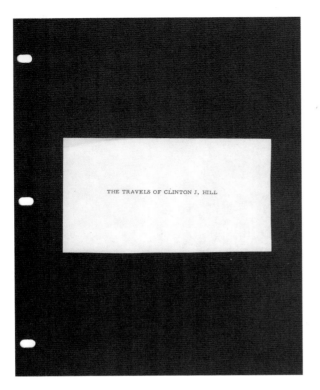

PAKISTAN -- Again in the background

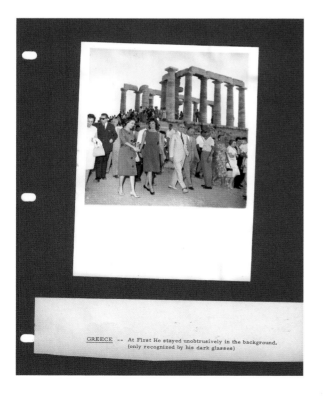

GREECE -- At First He stayed unobtrusively in the background.
(only recognized by his dark glasses)

ITALY -- Lurking in shadowy corners

ITALY -- Musical accompaniment to the pull of the oars

MOROCCO -- Taking care of the Press... "Keep smiling, Frances, because I am going to belt you. "

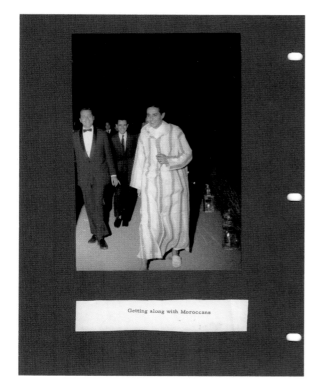

Getting along with Moroccans

SOMETIMES THERE WERE DUTIES AT HOME. Clint always tried to be there.

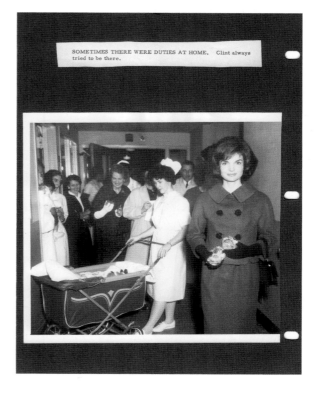

ANY PLACE -- Our able agents are always eager to serve

After a week of ten-hour days, Lisa and I had pretty much cleaned everything out. We had bags and boxes of items that would be donated, a stack of things we had packed up and would ship to our new home in California, and the dumpster in the driveway was nearly filled to the brim. I was going around checking every drawer and closet for the third and fourth time to make sure we weren't missing anything. As I walked around the basement, the sun was at such an angle that it was streaming through one of the small windows, casting a column of light into the open door of the closet under the stairs. I thought I had emptied everything, but sure enough, there was yet another nondescript brown cardboard box shoved way back in the corner that I had somehow missed.

I pulled out the box and carried it over to the desk. Inside were two black velvet flip-top boxes. I opened up the larger of the two, and there it was: a gold medal stamped with the U.S. Treasury seal and the words EXCEPTIONAL SERVICE IN THE TREASURY DEPARTMENT around the outer edge. Inside the smaller box was a replica, a pin to be worn on my lapel.

The Secret Service had had them encased in Lucite—I suppose so I could display them. On the back side of the medal was an etching of the U.S. Treasury building and the words: AWARDED TO CLINTON J. HILL, NOVEMBER 22, 1963.

I knew Lisa would be thrilled that I'd found them, but I had no sense of excitement or pleasure. I was simply relieved that the search was over. The medal was never anything I sought to receive or even wanted, because I still had this sense of guilt for not having fulfilled our obligation to protect the president. I have always felt this way.

Even though I've talked and written about the assassination for more than ten years, since meeting Lisa in 2009, and have managed to come to an acceptance of what happened, it still made me feel somewhat sick in my gut when I saw the medal. It was a reminder of a tragic day in U.S. history in which I had a part.

November 22, 1963, is a date I shall never forget and one, sadly, that I must live with for the rest of my life. For me there is no pride in what I did that day. While others may find my actions heroic, I consider them inadequate. No matter the praise I receive, I continue to have that sense of not having fulfilled my responsibility.

Eleven days after the assassination, December 3, 1963, Secretary of the Treasury Douglas Dillon presents me with the Treasury Department's highest civilian award for bravery as Mrs. Kennedy looks on, standing next to my two sons, Chris (7) and Corey (2), and my wife, Gwen. Behind Mrs. Kennedy are Assistant Secretary Robert A. Wallace and Mrs. Kennedy's secretary, Mary Gallagher.

When the award was presented to me on December 3, 1963, my wife, Gwen, brought my two young sons, Chris and Corey, to the ceremony in the Treasury Building. I didn't expect Mrs. Kennedy to be there, but shortly before the presentation began, she walked in, accompanied by Lee and her sisters-in-law Jean Kennedy Smith and Pat Kennedy Lawford.

For the previous three years, I had spent more time with her and her children than with my own wife and kids. We had traveled the world together and shared moments and memories that I had never shared with my wife. It was my job, but it had become so much more than that. That ceremony was the first and only time my wife and Mrs. Kennedy ever met.

She could have stood in the background, far out of the photographs, but she walked up to the podium with purpose and stood by my side. Just eleven days after the assassination, we were still numb, still drowning in grief. But Mrs. Kennedy had gotten dressed that day and had come to stand by my side.

In May 1994, nineteen years after I was retired, I got a call from Dave Carpenter, who was the Special Agent in Charge of Presidential Protection at that time. He told me that President Bill Clinton had asked about me and wanted to meet me. I had no idea why, but when the president of the United States wants to meet you, you go. Most people never have that opportunity.

The appointment was arranged for Thursday, May 19. From the moment I walked through the west entrance with Dave Carpenter, it felt so comfortable. I knew every inch of the White House, and while there had been quite a few different occupants since I was last there, not much else had changed.

At the appointed time, I went into the Oval Office and met President Clinton. After we shook hands, he said, "Mr. Hill, I'm sure you are aware that Mrs. Onassis is quite ill."

"Yes," I said. I couldn't bear to refer to her as Mrs. Onassis. To me she will forever be Mrs. Kennedy. "I am aware of the news reports that she has non-Hodgkin's lymphoma."

"Sadly," he said, "we have learned that her condition is extremely critical and deteriorating. I wanted to personally thank you for your service to her and for your distinguished career with the Secret Service."

We spoke for about ten or fifteen minutes about what a great lady she was and shared our individual memories with her, and then I left.

It was very thoughtful and kind of President Clinton to make the effort to tell me the sad news in person. Indeed, Mrs. Kennedy died that evening in her home at 1040 Fifth Avenue. Tears filled my eyes when I turned on the television the next morning and saw John F. Kennedy Jr. speaking to reporters.

"Last night at around ten fifteen, my mother passed on. She was surrounded by her friends and her family and her books, and the people and the things that she loved. And she did it in her own way, and in her own terms, and we all feel lucky for that. And now she's in God's hands."

The next day, I got a phone call from Jack Walsh, the Secret Service agent I had assigned to protect John and Caroline when I left the Kennedy Protective Detail in late 1964. Jack had stayed with John until he was sixteen years old and had become almost a member of the family.

We talked about what a sad day it was.

"How are John and Caroline holding up?" I asked.

"As well as can be," he said. "It's been tough. But they're strong. That's why I'm calling, Clint. The kids asked me to invite you to the interment at Arlington."

"Really?" I was stunned. I hadn't seen or talked to John or Caroline since leaving Mrs. Kennedy in 1964.

"Yes," Jack said, his voice now choking up a bit, "they said, 'Mummy always spoke so highly of Mr. Hill.' "

I swallowed hard, hoping my voice wouldn't crack as I spoke. "That's very nice to hear. I'd be honored to attend."

"The interment is going to be very small, very private. Mostly family and President and Mrs. Clinton. I'll get back to you with more details."

There were lots of phone calls over the next twenty-four hours, and, as is typical with these last-minute, high-profile but private ceremonies, the logistics were fluid. Nancy Tuckerman, who had remained a loyal assistant to Mrs. Kennedy all these years, was coordinating everything, and she filled me in on the specifics of what was happening and when. The funeral Mass was being held at the Church of St. Ignatius Loyola in Manhattan, and then the family was flying with the casket on a chartered jet to Washington for the burial at Arlington National Cemetery.

I had been invited to meet the family at National Airport and ride with President and Mrs. Clinton in the motorcade, but in the end, I drove myself to Secret Service headquarters and rode with the director of the Secret Service to Arlington National Cemetery.

It was early afternoon and the sun was blazing down, with not a cloud in the sky. Just like the last time I was there, honoring President Kennedy's birthday, thirty years earlier, almost to the day.

The pallbearers carried the flower-draped casket containing Mrs. Kennedy's body from the hearse and laid her gently onto the grass, in the reserved space next to President John Fitzgerald Kennedy. As Caroline and John led the procession of family and close friends to gather around the gravesite, the Eternal Flame, lit by their mother to honor their slain father, danced vibrantly, even in the bright light of day.

Fewer than one hundred people were in attendance at this somber ceremony, and everyone had been told where to stand. John and Caroline were of course front and center, with Caroline's husband, Edwin Schlossberg, and Mrs. Kennedy's longtime companion, Maurice Tempelsman, next to them. I waited in the back as President and Mrs. Clinton and the family members took their places, looking around at all the familiar faces: Mrs. Kennedy's sister Lee; Senator Ted Kennedy; Ethel; three of the Kennedy sisters—Jean Kennedy Smith, Patricia Kennedy Lawford, and Eunice Kennedy Shriver—along with their spouses, children, and grandchildren; Nancy Tuckerman; Eve and Paul Fout from Middleburg; and Provi with her son, Gustavo.

Jack had told me I was to stand in the front row of the semicircle, next to Provi, but I waited and filed in at the end, moving to the back, behind Maria Shriver and her husband, Arnold Schwarzenegger.

After welcoming remarks by the officiating archbishop, President Clinton walked to the podium.

"We are joined here today at the site of the Eternal Flame, lit by Jacqueline Kennedy Onassis thirty-one years ago, to bid farewell to this remarkable woman whose life will forever glow in the lives of her fellow Americans. Whether she was soothing a nation grieving for a former president, or raising the children with the care and privacy they deserve, or simply being a good friend, she seemed always to do the right thing, in the right way."

He spoke about her dedication as a mother and her love of history and art. He didn't speak long, but it was heartfelt. When he finished, John walked up to the podium and read a passage from the Bible.

As he read from the page in front of him, speaking with ease and eloquence, I felt like a proud uncle. I was there when he was born, and even though I'd left when he was almost four, I'd watched along with the rest of the world as he went through the typical phases of awkward adolescence and rebellious teenage years. Now here he was, a handsome, articulate young man, standing with great poise in this most difficult of circumstances.

Caroline had always been more quiet and reserved than John, but she had grown into a remarkable woman, now a wife and mother herself. As she read Psalm 121, I could sense that she would rather not have been in the spotlight, but she delivered the short verse flawlessly.

When the service concluded, I didn't linger. I walked quietly back to the car without speaking to anybody. I don't think anyone realized who I was or that I was even there.

But it meant something to me to be by her side that one last time.

May 23, 1994: I was honored to be invited to Jacqueline Kennedy Onassis's burial service at Arlington National Cemetery. I had been told to stand in the front row, but I felt more comfortable in the back. That's me, upper left, behind Arnold Schwarzenegger. Also at left are Teddy Kennedy, First Lady Hillary Clinton, President Bill Clinton, and Maria Shriver. John and Caroline stand next to Maurice Tempelsman. Provi is in the center of the photo, wiping her eyes, wearing a red and blue scarf.

People often ask me,
"What was Jackie Kennedy
really like?"
Well, now you know.

ACKNOWLEDGMENTS

The idea for this book came during the restrictive COVID-19 lockdowns in 2020. Writing, curating the photographs, and going through all the memorabilia was a wonderful distraction, and it also provided an opportunity to connect with friends from the past. While most of the narrative is based on Clint's personal recollections, we are grateful to former Secret Service agents Paul Rundle, Ron Pontius, Paul Landis, and Tom Wells for sharing their notes, photographs, and memories to fill in some of the gaps.

Additionally, our friend and retired Secret Service Agent Barbara Riggs was immensely helpful in connecting us with Stirling Young, Nina Fout, and photographer Howard Allen's daughters, Page Allen and Betsy Allen Davis, all of whom provided additional color to the Middleburg section. We are especially grateful to Page and Betsy for allowing us to use some of their father's wonderful photographs.

From the beginning, Keith Urbahn and Matt Latimer at Javelin have been as passionate about this book as we are. Their patience, integrity, and professionalism through negotiations, snafus, delays, and the many iterations of the book jacket were invaluable. We are so fortunate to have them in our corner. Likewise, we don't know what we'd do without the brilliant insight of Mitchell Ivers. We are grateful for his encouragement, guidance, spot-on advice, and most of all, his friendship.

Our partnership with Gallery Books goes back to 2010 and, once again, the talented team led by the incomparable Jen Bergstrom has turned our vision into a stunning book that will stand the test of time. We are grateful to Aimée Bell for believing in this book from the outset and for steering us through uncharted waters, and to Jennifer Long and Jen Robinson, who work tirelessly on our behalf. Additionally, we are thankful to everyone who worked behind the scenes: Carolyn Levin, Abby Zidle, Caroline Pallotta, Emily Arzeno, Allison Green, Gaitana Jaramillo, Jamie Selzer, John Vairo, Matthew Ryan, Chelsea McGuckin, Alexis Leira, Paul O'Halloran, Fiona Sharp, and Annie Wiese. Andrew Nguyễn was enormously helpful as liaison, assisting with the complex task of organizing 220 photographs and overall keeping us on track. And special thanks to the talented Lisa Litwack for creating the most gorgeous book jacket we've ever seen.

Thank you to Andy Howick at mptv Images, David Shaw, Maryrose Grossman at the JFK Library, Aline Lauvergeon at Photo12, and Michael Shulman at Magnum Photos.

Finally, we are so fortunate to have a priceless collection of friends and family members who offered suggestions and provided support along the way. Thank you to Chris, Corey, Cooper, Connor, and Abby; Wyman and Gay Harris; Stephanie Ryder; Liz McNeil; Pilar Proctor; Elaine Petrocelli; Mary Potuznik; Paige Peterson; Wendy Miller; Claire McAuliffe; and Faith Wheeler; and a special acknowledgment to John Lamar for the last-minute, totally perfect suggestion to add "My" to the title. We love you all!

PHOTOGRAPH CREDITS